"If Time Is Money, No Wonder I'm Not Rich"

The Busy Investor's Guide to Successful Money Management

Mary L. Sprouse

Simon & Schuster
New York London Toronto Sydney Tokyo Singapore

SIMON & SCHUSTER
Simon & Schuster Building
Rockefeller Center
1230 Avenue of the Americas
New York, New York 10020

Designed by Irving Perkins Associates
Manufactured in the United States of America

10 9 8 7 6 5 4 3 2 1

Library of Congress Cataloging-in-Publication Data
Sprouse, Mary L.
    "If time is money, no wonder I'm not rich" : the busy
investor's guide to successful money management /
Mary L. Sprouse
        p.   cm.
    Includes index.
    1. Finance, Personal.   2. Investments.   3. Time management.
I. Title.
HG179.S5578   1993
332.024—dc20
                                                92–37025
                                                    CIP

ISBN: 0-671-75160-3

for Maya

Contents

Chapter 5

Ten Timeless Investment Strategies 79

If you can duck through an alley, why hike around the block? To invest your earnings by the fastest route, use these smart money shortcuts, from payroll deduction and dividend reinvestment plans to asset management accounts and dollar-cost averaging.

Chapter 6

Ten Safe Investments You Can Make in Twenty Minutes or Less 103

Why savings bonds are worth a second look, mutual funds win the game of one-upmanship, Ginnie Maes make home mortgages an innovative investment, zero-coupon bonds are clever college savers, and more.

Chapter 7

How to Build Wealth Without Spending a Second or a Cent 143

A dollar saved at 8 percent today will be worth $8,426,588 in 2193. Okay, maybe you won't live that long—but the value of your dollar in thirty years is nothing to sneeze at, either. Discover five easy strategies for piggy-banking your way to wealth.

Chapter 8

Fast-Track Financial Professionals 154

No time to spare? Hordes of advisers will sell you theirs. To help you find and manage the best, here's the lowdown on every professional eager to whisper hot tips in your ear, from lawyers, stockbrokers, and insurance agents to tax preparers, financial planners, and money managers.

Chapter 1

Introduction: Money Management for Rush Hours

If there's life in outer space, one intergalactic sound must baffle them. A sound like a runaway metronome. The sound of America ticking.

Maybe you've been too busy to notice. But time has become the obsession of the age—as sought after and scarce as Shangri-la or sunken galleons.

"I'd love to, but I don't have time" has replaced "Let's do lunch" as the sign-off of the nineties. Stress now tops the list of mental afflictions. Workaholism is a socially acceptable addiction. And leisure is as endangered as the California condor.

Twenty years ago futurists predicted that automation would set us free. But technology has turned out to be a time bandit. The faster our machines turn out work, the more we're expected to do. Faxes demand immediate attention. Customers want next day delivery. The rhythms of computers are replacing the rhythms of natural life. With the world spinning faster and faster, most of us feel as though we're standing still.

To keep up, we start work earlier and return home later than ever before. We put in 46.8 hours a week—an increase of 6.2 hours over the last fifteen years. Professionals average 52.2 hours a week; small-business owners slave 57.3 hours.

Too bad no one's at home to handle daily chores. Instead two-earner couples and single parents must squeeze grocery shopping and laundry into evenings and weekends. The result: leisure time has shrunk to 16.2 hours a week, down from 26.2 hours in 1973.

Is it any wonder we can't find time for our money? Long workdays, lengthy commutes, and growing families already consume nearly every waking hour. Many Americans say they could work seven days a week, twenty-four hours a day, and not get everything done.

All the time you spend making money will be wasted, however, if you don't take time to manage it. Of all the activities you must cram into your busy life, managing your money is the one you can least afford to overlook. You can skip the vacuuming, put off wallpapering, miss a week of "Monday Night Football." No harm done. Let money management slide, however, and you may deprive yourself and your family of a home, quality education, and a secure, comfortable retirement.

The biggest mistake you can make with money is neglect. You might as well leave your dollar bills outside in a high wind. The dangers come in many guises:

- You deposit your paychecks in your checking account and forget about them. As a result, your account balance is always over $2,500. Your money earns no interest, and while your back is turned, inflation is gnawing away at your $2,500 like a fox who's sneaked into the henhouse.

- You let your receipts pile up during the year without categorizing and filing them. The mess is so intimidating that you put off filing your tax return. Because you've no idea whether you owe tax, you file for an extension without making any payment. When you finally sort out your records in October, you discover you owe $3,500. The unnecessary late payment penalty is over $500.

- Acting on a tip, you buy 1,000 shares of stock in a small-growth company at $5 a share. Three months later the company wins a government contract, and the price of a share shoots up to $8. Buried in paperwork when you're not imprisoned in traffic, you fail to check the stock quotes in your newspaper and miss out on a $3,000 gain.

Five months later the company comes under investigation for falsifying inspections tests, and the stock plummets to $.68 a share. Your loss is $4,320.

- To stay ahead of inflation, you shift $50,000 from a savings account to a brokerage firm. Feeling too pressed for time to make investment decisions, you open a discretionary account, giving your broker authority to make trades without your prior consent. You go back to your thriving family business, and the unopened monthly statements pile up on a hall table.

Four months later you learn that your $50,000 has dwindled down to $24,000. You also realize the broker has been churning your account, making sixty-six trades and raking in commissions of $14,000. Your business suffers while you meet with lawyers, trying to get your money back.

- A friend tells you about a limited partnership being formed to build budget motels. Your friend hands you the seventy-five-page prospectus, but quarterly reports are due at the office and you never get around to reading it. Trusting your friend's judgment, you put up $10,000 for two units.

If you'd looked at the prospectus, you'd have seen that the general partners' management fee limits the return on your investment to 4 percent at best. In your previous investment, your $10,000 had been earning 8.5 percent.

So what if there are crumbs under your toaster and cobwebs on your stack of professional journals? So what if you said "Let's do this again sometime" five years ago? You must make time for your money.

Easy to say. But where will this time magically come from? How about taking a slice out of the five years of your life you spend waiting in line (statistic from Michael Fortino of Priority Management Pittsburgh, a consulting firm)? Or from the six years you spend eating, the year searching for misplaced objects, or the two years trying to return phone calls from people who are never in?

Seriously, though, it's a question of setting priorities. Somehow we always find time for the urgent or the pleasurable. If the president can find time to play golf, you can make room for one more activity in your busy life. A crass, bothersome, and often tedious addition, to be sure. But a vital one.

At the stroke of midnight on New Year's Day 1988, scientists added one second to the world's clock. I can't perform a similar feat and add hours to your day. But I can help you make the most of the wee time you have.

This book is your guide to making and managing your money in the most efficient way possible. You'll find out how to simplify your financial life by applying time management principles to your personal finances. You'll learn smart money shortcuts—ten quick investing techniques that put your money to work for you. For those who want to get started yesterday, there are investments that will put you on the road to financial success in just twenty minutes. And for the long-range planner in all of us, there's a chapter on the time value of money and the effortless power of savings.

Because it pays to have a road map first, there's a quick primer on financial planning to help you set basic goals and go from zero-coupon bonds to sixty-month CDs in under an hour. You also get a crash course in investment principles, so you can map out a strategy that keeps on trucking even if you take your hands off the wheel.

If you want to buy time, you'll find out how to choose premium financial professionals and oversee their performance. In a separate chapter you'll learn how to turn your computer into a personal money manager and what software to enlist as your ally. And you'll discover how to save time and money on your taxes through a system of rapid record keeping.

Making and managing money on a tight schedule is not without its price. Hiring professional help is costly, and like gas-guzzling sports cars, investments designed for speed don't always produce the highest yield. Moreover, you can't even enjoy the leisure of being completely uninvolved. No matter how brilliant your advisers or fail-safe your investments, you still must be responsible for your financial affairs. It's your money, and the more you entrust it to someone else, the less you may have left.

Quick investing may not bring you quick riches. But, with the help of this guide, you can ensure a secure future for you and your family. With security comes financial independence—and all the time in the world.

Chapter 2

Organize Your Way to Fiscal Fitness

Most of us spend the least time on the things we value most. Surveys show that married couples spend about four minutes a day in meaningful conversation and working couples spend just thirty *seconds* a day talking with their children. And you think you'll find time to manage your money, too?

The fact is, our runaway lives don't leave much time for finance. But that doesn't mean your money has to gather dust, while time whisks you toward retirement, knee deep in bills and bank statements. The key is to simplify. The same time management principles that work in the office serve just as well at home. In this chapter we're going to hack through the jumble, blaze financial shortcuts, and square off against time in a classic showdown. When the smoke clears, I promise you'll be marshal of the slickest, most orderly finances around.

SIMPLIFY YOUR FINANCIAL LIFE

It's time to get organized. Stamp out clutter, and you'll save at least thirty minutes a day. Time once lost rummaging can be used to translate a prospectus into English, track the yield on money market funds, or, if you insist, watch "The Simpsons."

CLUTTER BUSTING

Buy a file cabinet. You have too many records to keep in a box under the bed. You'll need at least one four-drawer cabinet. If you don't buy a full-suspension cabinet, remember that pulling out the top drawer may cause it to topple like King Kong off the Empire State Building.

Now buy a supply of file folders and use them. Make a list of investment topics that interest you, such as stocks, money market funds, home buying, and collectibles. Devote a folder to newspaper clippings and magazine articles about each of these subjects as well. Resist the urge to collect information about every aspect of finance. If you're certain the commodities market will never tempt you, why waste time and space on it?

Your tax records for the current year also need to be categorized. The special record keeping required by the IRS is covered in chapter 10.

Don't subdivide your topics into a thicket of categories. You're not classifying flora and fauna. Keep categories broad to speed research. For example, one folder labeled "Stocks" is all you need for stock-related articles. Only when a file becomes too full should you branch out into subfiles, such as dollar-cost averaging, short selling, and blue chips.

Choose categories that spring readily to mind. If you think of your Honda as a "car," don't create an "automobile" file. Thumb through your files from time to time to jog your memory and avoid duplication. For example, you might find a file labeled "Insurance—

Life" and one marked "Life Insurance." You might also discover that the article on college costs for which you dutifully made a "College" folder could have been quickly filed under "Education."

FINANCIAL CATEGORIES CHECKLIST

What subjects are you likely to need? Here are a few suggestions:

Banking	Insurance—Health
Bonds	Insurance—Life
Brokers	Insurance—Other
Business Opportunities	Money Market Funds
Certificates of Deposit	Municipal Bonds
Credit	Pension Plans
Diversification	Record Keeping
Education	Rental Real Estate
Employee Benefits	Saving
Estate Planning	Stock
Financial Planning	Taxes
Financing Home Ownership	U.S. Gov't. Securities

Your aim is fast, not flash. Label folders by hand, using ink or a fine-point felt marker. Your typed label will hide it later if perfectionism wins out. Don't worry about staggering the tabs. As the folders fill up, the tabs will stand out clearly, even if they're all on one side or in the middle.

File alphabetically. A numeric or color-coded system may be perfect for Smiley's people, but the Cold War's over, and you want a system anyone can understand. After all, you may want to delegate this chore someday. An index is another time waster.

Hanging files are lovely to look at and murder to own. They overrun your drawer space, smother your files, and slump like wet laundry. Shun them. Your folders will stand by themselves in your file drawers just fine without them.

Now, in a burst of energy, file everything on hand. Then keep up with it. Sort financial records and materials regularly. Jot the categories in the upper right-hand corners if you don't have time to file immediately or if you're delegating this joyful task.

Date clippings and literature. Financial articles quickly become obsolete as economic conditions and tax laws change. Purge your files at least once a year, discarding outdated material, such as articles touting once top-performing mutual funds or recommending home refinancing based on short-lived mortgage rates.

Keep tax records, however, for at least three years. At year end relegate the past year's records to a lower drawer, and set up folders for the new year. Move older tax records to storage boxes.

Discard expired insurance policies and records of real estate or major purchases you no longer own.

Store valuable legal documents, such as birth and marriage certificates, stock certificates, deeds, insurance policies, and your will in a safety deposit box at your bank. This is also a good place to keep an inventory and photographs of your valuables—in case they're stolen or destroyed by fire. Keep photocopies of important documents in your file cabinet at home.

Finally, spring for in and out baskets. Don't let them collapse under their own weight, however. That will only intimidate you. Write checks for bills when received, and balance checkbooks monthly. Try to cluster due dates around the same time. For example, arrange for your house, car, and recreational vehicle payments to be payable on the first or fifteenth of every month. Invest in certificates of deposit that mature near the same date. Minimize installment payments, and interest expense, by paying off charges at once.

To alert you to matters requiring action, such as postdated checks waiting to be mailed, set up a home version of the suspense or "tickler" file lawyers use. To keep it simple, we're going to limit the file to the next two months. You need two file folders, one for each month, with the current month in front. Behind the current month's file, add four files for each week of the month. File documents or projects according to the week you must start work on them, not the deadline. At the end of the month, transfer the now empty week files to the next month, and start over.

MAINTAIN A FINANCIAL CALENDAR

No meeting in America can take place until it has the blessing of our appointment books. So why shouldn't your finances be subject to the same discipline? After all, a reminder to make a regular contribution to Junior's college fund is as helpful as penciling in that power breakfast with Giantco's director of sales.

Use a calendar that shows one month at a time. Post it in your work area. Enter important deadlines, such as the due date of your mortgage payment. Besides preventing late charges, a glance at the month ahead will help you budget for extraordinary expenses, such as your property tax bill or vehicle registration.

Now schedule time to attend to specific financial tasks—reviewing your mutual fund's track record, for example, or reading investment publications. To avoid scheduling conflicts, enter these "appointments" in your business calendar as well.

BUILDING SPEED

Let's not fool around. Let's go for the gold and win the financial Olympics hands down. The fastest money manager, like the fastest swimmer, is the one who takes the least strokes.

Where does that championship ability come from? It comes from training, practice, inspired coaching, and top-notch facilities. So before the starter gun goes off, I recommend the following.

ACQUIRE FINANCIAL SKILLS

There's no point in wringing minutes from your schedule, like moisture from a cactus, unless you know what to do with them. Until you know the basics of investing, financial planning, and money management, your time will seep away like water out of a spilled canteen.

Here's where you have to *spend* time to save time. But the yield on your initial investment in learning will be impressive. It will speed your reading and understanding of technical materials, improve your financial judgment, and enable you to make quick, but sound, investment decisions.

Your coaches? Begin with financial magazines. There are about a dozen on the newsstands. General advice on popular financial topics, such as home buying and retirement planning, can be found in *Money* and *Kiplinger's Personal Finance* magazine. For sophisticated investors there are *Barron's, Forbes, Financial World*, and *BusinessWeek*, to name a few. To begin, buy six different magazines, skim through their indices, and read the lead articles. Then subscribe to two or three that seem helpful.

If you're interested in stock trading, you may want to

subscribe to an investment newsletter. These can cost up to $250 a year, so the best place to start is probably your local library. Review several issues for risk posture and clarity. Many newsletters provide a free sample on request or, at least, a trial subscription at a reduced rate. Select Information Exchange (212-874-6408) will send your choice of fifteen sample letters for $7.97. The monthly *Hulbert Financial Digest* ranks 110 newsletters on performance (316 Commerce St., Alexandria, VA 22314, $37.50 for a five-month trial, or try your library).

Other useful investment guides to look for in your library are the *Value Line Investment Survey* and *Standard & Poor's Common Stock Reports* for stocks and *Mutual Fund Sourcebook* and *Wiesenberger Investment Companies Services* for mutual funds. These publications detail the earnings records and business outlook of stocks and the track record of funds.

Send away for advertised information—about mutual funds, financial software, and investment newsletters, for example. Tear out the names and addresses of free or inexpensive publications mentioned in magazine articles, and write a one- or two-line letter requesting a copy. Write for annual reports of companies featured in *Forbes* and *Inc.* magazines. Ask to be placed on the mailing list for government consumer publications (Consumer Information Center, Pueblo, CO 81009).

Brokerage firms offer a wealth of free investment advice. Merrill Lynch, for example, gives away a thirty-page booklet entitled *How to Read a Financial Report* and *Short-Term Fixed-Income Investments,* a brochure discussing Treasury bills, money market securities, and commercial paper. Coopers & Lybrand will send you *Guide to Financial Instruments* (1251 Avenue of the Americas, New York, NY 10020).

Other sources of free and useful advice include the twelve Federal Reserve Banks. For instance, the Dallas

Federal Reserve publishes a bimonthly economic fore-
cast in its *Dallas Fed Economic Review* (Public Affairs Department, Station K, Dallas, TX 75222). The St. Louis
Fed offers data on interest rates and money growth in
its monthly *Monetary Trends* report and weekly *U.S. Financial Data* booklet (Public Information Office, P.O. Box
442, St. Louis, MO 63166). From the Federal Reserve in
New York comes *The Arithmetic of Interest Rates, Basic
Information on Treasury Bills,* and *How to Read U.S. Government Securities Quotes* (Public Information Department, 33 Liberty Street, New York, NY 10045).

Interested in precious metals? The Gold Institute will
gladly send you its pamphlet, *Your Introduction to Investing in Gold* (Administrative Office, Suite 101, 1026 Sixteenth St. NW, Washington, D.C. 20036). The Silver
Institute at the same address will ship you its bimonthly
newsletter at no charge. Both publications are essen-
tially sales brochures, but they do offer a good introduction to their subjects.

The American Association of Retired Persons puts out
Take Charge of Your Money, which includes worksheets
and strategies to help you make the most of your assets
(AARP, P.O. Box 2240, Long Beach, CA 90801).

Snatch a half hour of financial advice on television
from time to time. Tune in to CNBC, the financial network; "Wall Street Week," "Nightly Business Report,"
and "Adam Smith's Money World" on PBS; "Your
Money" and "MoneyWeek" on CNN; or the local
business report on your nightly news. Ignore strictly
commercial programs on cable channels that masquer-
ade as investment advice while trying to enlist you in
direct marketing schemes or sell you seminars or tapes
promising easy riches.

Read the business section of your newspaper, especially on Sunday. Buy *The Wall Street Journal* one day a
week if you're passing a newsstand.

Build a reference library. Not books you're going to sit right down and read cover to cover. Books you can dip into whenever you want to know how an index fund works, for example, or how market timers pick stocks, or what factors to consider in buying real estate. Of course, if you do find time to read *The Money Game* or some other tome all the way through, you'll have that much greater an advantage.

Read the regular book reviews in *BusinessWeek*, and look for the year-end lists of best business books in magazines and newspapers. Remember, though, that investment books dealing with current economic conditions are often out of date before they see print. Your core library should consist of books that treat finance and investments generally or that time has proven to be classics, such as

- *Extraordinary Popular Delusions and the Madness of Crowds*, Charles Mackay (Harmony Books)
- *A Random Walk Down Wall Street*, Burton Malkiel, (W. W. Norton)
- *The Money Game*, Adam Smith (Random House)
- *The Battle for Investment Survival*, Gerald Loeb (Fraser Publishing Company)
- *The Common Sense Mortgage*, Peter G. Miller (Harper & Row)
- *Money Angles* and *The Only Investment Guide You'll Ever Need*, Andrew Tobias (Avon and Bantam)
- *Sylvia Porter's Your Finance in the 1990s*, Sylvia Porter (Prentice-Hall)
- *J. K. Lasser's Real Estate Investment Guide*, Gary Barr with Judith Headington McGee (J. K. Lasser Institute)
- *One Up on Wall Street*, Peter Lynch with John Rothchild (Simon & Schuster)

- *Plan Your Estate,* Denis Clifford (Nolo Press)
- *The Money Masters,* John Train (Harper & Row)

Now that you've assembled a coaching staff, your training program can begin. The only limits are your enthusiasm and, of course, your time. But if you advance no farther, you should at least learn

- to read the stock table in your newspaper
- to understand a mutual fund or limited partnership prospectus
- to speed-read corporate annual reports
- to recognize the difference between simple and compound interest
- to compute your net worth (I'll show you how in chapter 4)
- to read a balance sheet and profit-and-loss statement
- to distinguish the characteristics and mechanics of popular investment vehicles (annuities, bonds and debentures, discounted mortgages, stock and money market mutual funds, options, real estate investment trusts, stocks)
- to understand the definition of common financial terms, such as book value, closed- vs. open-end fund, common vs. preferred stock, leverage, load, margin, par, price-earnings ratio, short sale, stop loss, and yield
- to become familiar with various economic terms and historically important concepts, such as supply and demand, gross national product, consumer price index, Keynesian economics, monetarism, supply-side economics, and new classical economics
- to comprehend the effects of inflation and recession on the economy and the performance of different investments

- to manage basics of the tax law and the Form 1040
- to operate a financial calculator

MAKE THE MOST OF YOUR TIME

You must manage your time as effectively as you manage your money. That means being in the starting block when the gun goes off and gaining the most ground with every stride. Here's how to make sure you're first across the finish line:

■ **Make money management a habit.** Set aside a couple of hours a week to tackle financial tasks. Don't look for large blocks of time. Try to grab half an hour every day if that's all you can manage.

Establishing a routine will actually enlarge your time. As the essayist and novelist May Sarton writes, "Routine is not a prison, but the way into freedom from time. The apparently measured time has immeasurable space within it."

If you practice a little money management every day, it will be easy to pick up financial tasks where you left off. You won't waste time refreshing your memory or retracing your steps.

■ **Have a plan.** List your financial duties and objectives in order of priority and the steps you must take to accomplish them. This will focus your thoughts and reduce start-up time.

Draw up a master list of weekly tasks, and schedule them on your calendar. Stick to your schedule. Don't let yourself be sidetracked.

■ **Break tasks into parts.** If meeting one of your objectives seems overwhelmingly like running a financial marathon, don't quail. Break down your goal into manageable activities. Outline each step, and estimate how

---

BALANCING YOUR CHECKBOOK ON THE RUN

- Record all deposits and checks, including ATM transactions, and keep a running total as you go.
- Mark off canceled checks and deposits in your check register. Don't stop to put checks in numerical order.
- Begin reconciling from the balance you show for the last canceled check—don't add up checks that haven't yet cleared the bank. For example, if check number 850 is the last one included with your statement, don't skip down to your balance on the day you wrote check 864.
- Add deposits made and subtract checks written before the date of the last canceled check (in this case, check 850).
- Add/subtract the *net* interest and service charges shown on the statement.
- Compare the result with the ending balance shown on your statement.
- Don't worry about discrepancies of $10 or less. Assume the bank is right, and enter the corrected total.
- If you're in a big hurry, just make sure your deposits, checks, and ATM withdrawals are correct on the bank statement.
- Create a buffer zone by never dipping below the minimum balance required to avoid service charges.

---

long it will take to conquer it. Allow yourself a time cushion, for safety's sake.

Then begin with the easiest part.

- **Batch tasks.** For speed, batch related activities. Write all your checks on the first Sunday of the month, for example. Then drop them into your tickler file by mailing date, so your efficiency doesn't cost you interest.

Map out an itinerary to handle all your financial

chores while you're running other errands—stops at the bank and your stockbroker when you're out grocery shopping, for example.

■ **Expedite mail handling.** We spend eight months of our lives opening junk mail. Or you do. I toss mine out unopened and unmourned.

Open and sort mail daily into one of three categories: "To Do/Pay," "To Read," or "To File." Throw away envelopes and junk inserts. Learn to recognize your important mail and discard the rest. Remember, mail bearing a bulk rate stamp is either junk or a plea for contributions. If a piece of mail touting a financial product catches your eye, by all means, give it a glance. But never invest by mail. Put financial magazines in your "To Read" basket if you can't give them immediate attention.

■ **Eliminate distractions.** Don't try to reconcile your checkbook on your knee with your two-year-old tugging at your pant leg. Instead set up a well-lighted home office in a quiet corner. If your only space is the kitchen table, clear it completely and cordon off the area while you're working. See "The Perfect Home Office," page 34.

■ **Create portable work.** Time is elusive. Capturing spare moments can be like pinning down a fragment of a dream. The efficient money manager snatches every second before it evaporates into thin air.

For example, catch up on routine financial reading while waiting at your doctor's office. Watch business shows on television, or listen to financial books on tape during your commute.

Carry a minioffice with you. Organize your briefcase with folders labeled "To Do," "To Pay," "To Read." Add essential office supplies—paper clips, pens, Post-it notes, a stapler, stamps, plus anything else you use frequently (I always have a 1040 instruction booklet handy).

■ **Be decisive.** Weigh thoroughly the pros and cons of an investment, but not ad infinitum. "The only thing worse than a bad decision is indecision," says the quotable Professor Brown. Curb your perfectionism. It robs you of time—and money.

■ **Overcome buyer's remorse.** For some investors, it's always three o'clock in the morning. That's when those nagging doubts begin—did I pay too much, can I afford it, am I going to lose everything?

Some uncertainty is a normal part of investing. But a strong dose of buyer's remorse is counterproductive and eats up valuable time. To check needless regrets:

- Don't wait until *after* an investment to raise questions and doubts. Consider everything that could go wrong in the planning stage.
- Analyze why you want to make the investment to discover whether you're being pushed into a bad financial decision for the wrong reasons—because it's a status symbol, for example.
- Don't rush into buying. Major investments require research and evaluation.
- Consider the investment from various viewpoints. For instance, in buying a new home, imagine the questions your banker, a future buyer, or a builder might ask. These different perspectives will broaden your judgment and reduce your fears of overlooking impending disaster.

■ **Fight procrastination.** In England there's a saying: "One of these days is *none* of these days." The time to get started is now.

BANKING ON THE RUN

- Bank near your home or office.
- Pick a bank with extended banking hours and/or a twenty-four-hour hot line.
- Choose an uncrowded small or private bank for shorter lines and more personal service.
- Never visit the bank on Friday afternoons, weekends, or during lunch hour.
- Use the drive-up window or automated teller machine (ATM) for deposits and cash withdrawals.
- Deposit checks weekly, not daily.
- Deposit checks by mail.
- Order an endorsement stamp for checks to be deposited from one of the tellers.
- Use deposit slips with carbon copies. Write name of payee, not bank number, next to the amount.
- Withdraw enough cash to last a week or longer.
- Conserve cash by writing checks or paying with charge cards.
- Obtain an ATM card from a bank that is a member of a nationwide system such as Star or Cirrus.
- Choose the same personal identification number (PIN) for each ATM or credit card, if possible, for ease of memory.
- Arrange telephone transfer and wire redemption between your bank and your money market or stock mutual fund family.
- Limit bank accounts to one checking and one business account if single; one joint checking account if married (two separate accounts optional).
- Become acquainted with the bank manager and tellers.
- Have your driver's license handy when cashing a personal check.
- Make sure your signature card is on file at the branch where you bank if you opened your account elsewhere.
- Familiarize yourself with your bank's services.

CONSOLIDATE

You'll never win the time race taking two strokes for every one that's necessary. You'll be winded long before you reach your goal, because, in effect, you'll have gone twice the distance. You must conserve motion. You must consolidate.

- **Keep account numbers in one place.** Keep a notebook in which you list the name and number of every credit card and bank account, as well as the company's phone number. Or lay out all your credit cards and photocopy them onto one sheet of paper. Frankly, I also list my personal identification numbers (PINs), despite all advice to memorize them, then swallow the slips of paper. This saves me from punching in dozens of numbers like a felon every time I use an ATM. It also saves having to prove my identity to American Express or AT&T from phone booths in strange cities every few months in order to get a new PIN.
- **Bank accounts.** Combine bank accounts. If you're single, stick to one interest-bearing checking account, one money-market account, and one business account if you're self-employed.

If you're married, one joint checking account that pays interest and one money market account are all you need—even if you have different names. If you both want your own money, at least pay all household bills from one joint account.
- **Credit cards.** Pitch unneeded plastic. The average American adult now has eight credit cards. You can probably get by with two major credit cards, however—one for personal purchases and one for business. If you crave more purchasing power, ask for a higher credit limit. Besides fewer bills to pay, you'll save on annual fees.

If you can't kick the credit card habit that easily, at least discard cards on which you charge less than a fixed amount per year, say, $500.

■ **Streamline your investments.** Put your savings in no more than five money market or stock mutual funds. Or invest funds in long-term certificates of deposit that roll over automatically. Stagger the maturity dates at six-month intervals initially for liquidity: you'll have money coming due every six months if you need it.

Review your portfolio's performance at least annually, deciding which investments to hold or sell.

Some investments are more time-consuming than others. Commodities trading, for example, requires the vigilance of an air traffic controller. A passbook savings account needs no more attention than a corpse. Ten worry-free investments are discussed in chapter 6.

■ **Leave stocks and bonds with your broker.** Why waste a trip to your safety deposit box every time you want to sell shares? Your certificates can be held in your name at your brokerage firm or in "street name"—that is, with the broker listed as the shareholder. You merely have to call in your sell order, and it will be handled electronically by your broker.

There are pros and cons to letting your broker hold your stock in street name. On the plus side, the broker takes responsibility for safeguarding your certificates. Your shares are insured for up to $500,000 per account by the Securities Investor Protection Corporation (SIPC)—you have no such protection if you hold and store the shares in your name. Trades are also quick and easy. On the other hand, if your account is not actively traded, your broker may charge a custodial fee.

■ **Individual retirement accounts (IRAs).** If you make both deductible and nondeductible IRA contributions, invest them in separate accounts. You may find yourself in this situation if your adjusted gross income is more than $40,000 on a joint return ($25,000 single) and you or your spouse are covered by a pension plan where you work. In that case your deductible IRA contribution is reduced by $1 for every $5 of adjusted gross income over $40,000 joint ($25,000 single).

For example, Alan decides to make a $2,000 IRA contribution. Because the joint return he files with Jessica shows an adjusted gross income of $45,000, only one-half of his contribution is deductible. He deposits the deductible $1,000 in a money market fund and the other, nondeductible $1,000 in a bond mutual fund.

This will greatly simplify his bookkeeping when he begins withdrawing funds. Money he takes out of the bond mutual fund will not be taxed because contributions to it were not deductible. IRA funds withdrawn from the money market will be taxed, however, because they were previously deducted. If Alan's contributions had all gone into the same account, higher math would be needed to determine how much of each withdrawal should be taxed.

■ **Insurance.** Weed out unnecessary or overlapping insurance policies. Life insurance on your children's lives and accidental death and credit life insurance polices are among the expendable. Cash in miscellaneous smaller policies, and consolidate your coverage if you can do so without generating costly sales charges or commissions.

Buy all of your insurance from the same agent. Working through a single agent for auto, homeowner's, and liability insurance minimizes paperwork and avoids conflicts over which insurance covers a particular claim.

Ask your agent to quote you an all-inclusive rate or grant you a package discount.

■ **Student loans.** You may merge up to four categories of student loans and make payments with a single check. If your lenders don't offer this option to consolidate, call the Student Marketing Association and ask about its Smart Loan Program (800-524-9100).

- **Cut your number of payments.** You're free to turn down a favor, even if it comes on a silver platter. For instance, you can refuse the option of making installment payments for life and auto insurance premiums and real estate tax bills. This saves you the trouble of writing monthly or biannual checks, as well as the interest and service charges usually tacked on for processing.

THE RIGHT TOOLS

You could bang a nail in with a spoon—eventually. But your picture could be hung much faster with a hammer. By the same token, you could spend an ice age figuring your net worth with an abacus or take a nanosecond at your computer workstation.

- **The perfect home office.** Managing your money is a business. You may not have the profits or the payroll of IBM, but you have the same need for an office.

Set aside an area where you can work uninterrupted. You don't have to commandeer an entire room. Use a screen, bookcases, or filing cabinets to block off a portion of a room and discourage distractions.

Your desk should have at least one drawer to hold office supplies and one drawer for files. The most functional desk is a large board or door set on top of two small filing cabinets. Add a glass top for easy cleaning.

Build an L- or U-shaped work unit by adding an equipment table, credenza, or both at right angles to your desk. With everything you need at arm's reach, there will be no wasted motion.

■ **Reference books.** If you don't have room for a free-standing bookcase, install shelves above your work area. Use them to house your financial library, bulky items that won't fit in your filing cabinets, and reference books. Some of the reference works you may want to buy include

- *The Money Income Tax Handbook,* Mary L. Sprouse (Time-Warner)
- *Compound Interest Tables,* Michael Sherman (Contemporary Books)
- *Mortgage Payments,* Solomon, Marshall, Pepper (Barron's)
- *Dictionary of Finance and Investment Terms,* John Downes and Jordan Elliot Goodman (Barron's)

You may also want one of the mutual fund directories:

- *The Investor's Guide to Low-Cost Mutual Funds,* Mutual Fund Education Alliance, 1900 Erie St., Suite 120, Kansas City, MO 64116 ($5)
- *IBC/Donoghue's Money Fund Directory* and/or *Donoghue's Mutual Funds Almanac,* Donoghue Organization, 360 Woodland St., Box 8008, Holliston, MA 01746 ($27.95 for the directory, $34.95 for the almanac)
- *The Individual Investor's Guide to No-Load Mutual Funds,* American Association of Individual Investors, 625 N. Michigan Ave., Dept. NLG, Chicago, IL 60611 ($24.95)
- *The Handbook for No-Load Fund Investors,* Business One Irwin, 1818 Ridge Road, Homewood, IL 60430 ($34.95)

And to keep you organized and efficient, how about

- *Conquering the Paper Pile-Up,* Stephanie Culp (Writer's Digest Books)

- *How to File and Find It*, a free booklet available from the Quill Corporation Business Library, 100 Schelter Rd., Lincolnshire, IL 60069
- *How to Get Control of Your Time and Your Life*, Alan Lakein (Signet, New American Library)

■ **Office supplies.** Stock up on plenty of office supplies each time you buy. For one-stop shopping, visit one of the large office supply warehouses, such as Staples or Bizmart, or place a telephone order from such mail-order firms as Reliable (800-735-4000). Some office supply stores also deliver free of charge.

Order printed letterhead and envelopes to save time in mailing. Buy a stationery rack to hold your letterhead, forms, and envelopes, and place it near your desk.

Purchase a rubber stamp with your name and address for return mail envelopes.

Buy stamps by the roll. These can be ordered by mail and charged to your MasterCard or Visa (800-STAMP24). Invest in a postal scale to avoid lines at the post office.

■ **Equipment.** For routine financial tasks, an inexpensive pocket calculator will do nicely. If you graduate to more sophisticated computations, such as figuring the time value of money or a loan amortization, invest in a moderately priced financial calculator like the Hewlett Packard 12C or 10B, the Texas Instruments BA-III, or the Casio FC-100.

Of course, for speed, using a calculator instead of a personal computer is like competing at Le Mans in a Model T. Chapter 9 will discuss using a computer to manage money.

ADD HOURS TO THE DAY

It's an axiom of modern life: if you run out of land, build up. The same holds true for time. When all your spare moments are filled, your time may have to serve two purposes. Try these tactics for double-decking your day:

- **Use the telephone whenever possible.** If you're always on the road, install a car phone to keep in touch with your broker, apartment manager, and banker, as well as your office. Bank by phone—just press the right buttons and you can pay your bills, find out your balance, and learn about new financial services.
- **Deposit your paycheck automatically.** Take advantage of your employer's offer to deposit your wages directly into your bank account. To direct deposit a Social Security or other government check, fill out a form available at your bank or Social Security office.
- **Let your bank pay your bills.** Arrange for your bank to automatically transfer money out of your account into a payee's account at the right time each month. You can set this up through your mortgage lender, other lender, insurance company, or utility company by filling out a form and submitting a voided personal check. To guard against a bill being paid before you make a deposit, apply for overdraft protection. (Some banks charge a fee for this feature.)
- **Use check registers with carbon copies.** You won't have to bother with logging a separate entry.
- **Take advantage of twenty-four-hour financial services.** Choose a bank close to your home with a twenty-four-hour hot line and automated teller machine. Invest in a family of funds that gives portfolio information and yield and price quotes around the clock. Buy and sell

stocks through a twenty-four-hour brokerage firm such as Spear Securities.

- **Subscribe to a financial news and stock quote service.** For the price of a phone call, you can dial up daily reports and technical analyses of thousands of companies. Stock quote services include Stock Fone, Dow-Phone, and SchwabQuotes. Chapter 9 has more information.
- **Trade stocks from home.** With a personal computer, financial software, and a modem, you can buy and sell stocks directly from a number of discount brokers and banks. Fidelity (800-544-6666), Charles Schwab (800-334-4455), Citibank (800-248-4472), and Chase Manhattan (800-632-2515) all offer investor programs. Bear in mind that you're strictly on your own when trading by computer. There's no stockbroker or financial adviser to review your decisions.
- **Use a mortgage-rate reporting service to shop for a loan.** For a fast comparison of rates and terms, HSH Associates in Butler, NJ (800-873-2837), surveys lenders in about thirty states, including most major metropolitan areas ($20). The Gary Myers Report in Chicago (312-642-9000) covers fifteen cities ($20), and National Mortgage Weekly in Cleveland (216-273-6605) covers Cleveland, Columbus, and Detroit ($3).
- **Combine pleasure and profit.** Attend investment seminars on board a cruise ship or inspect rental and commercial properties while on vacation. Shop for antiques or art on a tour of Europe. (*Note:* Buy collectibles for enjoyment rather than for investment, unless you qualify as an expert. With luck you'll also turn a profit, but don't count on it as a key element in your financial plan.)
- **Delegate to your children.** Train and pay them to sort and add up canceled checks, for example, or to read

PAYING BILLS ON THE RUN

- Don't pay bills in person or by cash.
- Write checks for bills as soon as received. Use a tickler file for checks that aren't immediately due.
- Cluster payment due dates around the same time.
- Use a check register with carbon copies.
- Have your phone number printed on all checks.
- Write your account number and/or the nature of the expense on the memo line in the bottom left-hand corner of your checks. If you're paying two or more deductible expenses with one check, note the amount and nature of each (such as "Visa, $36.00 office supplies; $27.00 business gifts"). If paying income taxes, note your Social Security number, tax period, and type of tax.
- Write the check number and date paid on all bills or invoices.
- Use a rubber stamp to print your return address on payment envelopes. Order your stamp from an office supply store for around $8 ($13 preinked).
- Use your canceled check as your receipt.
- Use a check-writing service such as Quicken or Check-Free. Chapter 9 has more information on how computers can help you.
- Round up to the nearest zero when you pay credit card, utility, or other computer-generated bills (in other words, pay $75 if the bill is $74.95). Let the computer give you a credit toward the next payment.
- Reduce the number of payments you make by paying ahead on your utility and credit card bills (pay $100 to cover the next three months' gas bill). Write such checks only on a low-interest-bearing account.
- Make gas, grocery, clothing, and fast-food purchases with a debit card. The money is deducted automatically from your checking account. Use your card only where fees are minimal. Don't forget to record your transactions.

stock tables and graph the rise and fall of your stocks' prices every week.

▪ **Hire a professional.** An army of stockbrokers, accountants, lawyers, tax preparers, and financial planners stands waiting to answer your cry for help. In chapter 8 you'll learn how to choose the one best suited to your needs.

Chapter 3

The ABCs of Investing in One Easy Lesson

The Indy 500 is a test of skill, reflexes, and nerve. At two hundred miles an hour, a driver's attention can't waver for an instant. Even the fiercest concentration sometimes falters, however. Then a car slams into a wall and disintegrates in a ball of flame.

As a busy investor, you don't have time to watch the road as closely as a racing pro. The route you pick to reach your financial destination should be as straight as I-70 through Kansas, a road where you can put your investments on cruise control, confident you won't look up to find yourself hurtling toward Dead Man's Curve.

This chapter will help you map out an investment strategy that practically drives itself. Using this hands-off approach to investing, you can design a mix of investments that arrives at your financial goals by the quickest, surest route.

Of course, you can't fall asleep at the wheel. You should conduct a portfolio checkup at least once a year to make sure your investment vehicles are still on track and to make any necessary course corrections.

What goes into engineering a low-maintenance investment strategy? In this chapter we'll outline factors you should consider when making investment decisions. Then you'll learn to analyze investments at a glance and identify which best fit your financial plan. Finally, we'll rank all major investments, with emphasis on their time-saving properties.

A CUSTOM STRATEGY FOR HANDS-OFF INVESTING

It's not enough to know where you're headed. The route to your financial goals twists through a maze of investment choices. You need a road map to set you on the right highway. You need an investment strategy.

There's no Rand McNally of investment interstates and county truck roads, no atlas of blue highways to retirement or scenic routes to capital gains. That's because no two starting points are the same. The road you take depends upon such factors as your age, whether you're married, your saving and spending habits, your tax situation, even your temperament. So you must chart your own course and design an investment strategy that matches not only your busy life-style, but your investing personality, your hopes, and your fears.

Keep your strategy simple. Build in a few safety features, enough power to pass low-yielding investment vehicles, and, of course, cruise controls. Then fine-tune it, adding more sophisticated options as your experience and know-how increase.

Adopt specific tactics. For example, if stock market plunges make you jittery, but you like the growth potential of small stocks, part of your strategy might be to limit stock holdings to 20 percent of your invested assets.

You could spend the rest of your waking hours reading about investing techniques and financial products. All you'd find, however, is that every author has his own opinion, usually different from the rest. Therefore there's no reason to depend on others in formulating your strategy. Learn the basics of investing, then rely on your own judgment and common sense. Not only will you save time, you'll be able to put your financial plan in motion immediately.

GUIDELINES FOR MAPPING OUT A STRATEGY

Even if your strategy is as personalized as your license plate, it should be based on common principles. In plotting the path to your financial goals, consider the following.

TIME COMMITMENT

Investing money, not time, is what this book is all about. Don't adopt a portfolio that will devour your hours like some man-eating plant in an investment Shop of Horrors. Don't strap yourself into daredevil investments, like commodities, that will crash and burn if you turn your head for an instant. Use the chart at the end of this chapter to analyze how much time your investment plan will require.

SPECIAL SKILLS NEEDED

Profiting from investments like art collecting and rare coins calls for expert knowledge—knowledge gained only after long hours spent poring over dusty books, attending auctions and collectors' club meetings, and visiting dealers and galleries. Since time is at a premium, choose a strategy you can implement without getting a new diploma.

REASON FOR INVESTMENT AND DESIRED RATE OF RETURN

In chapter 4 you will develop a financial plan and compute the yield required to meet your goals (see pages 65–78). The best strategy aims directly for these objectives. Compare the purpose and rate of return of various investments before settling on your portfolio. Does an investment provide liquidity, current or future income, capital growth, safety of principal, or tax relief? How well do its characteristics match your goals? Determine the expense of buying, selling or liquidating each investment, including load fees, commissions, and tax cost. These costs reduce your yield.

RISK VERSUS REWARD

Risky investments promise greater profits but require close monitoring. A hands-off strategy, therefore, minimizes risk. This means a trade-off—higher yield is sacrificed for time savings. In analyzing investments, weigh the profit potential against the risk involved. Assess your ability to cope with losses both financially and mentally, and don't exceed your risk tolerance.

STAGE OF LIFE

Are you at a stage in life where your goal is to amass wealth? Or have you reached the age where you want to conserve it and live on the income? The first demands an offensive investment strategy; the latter calls for a defensive strategy.

An offensive strategy should be postponed, however, until you have saved enough to build a sound financial base that includes a home, insurance, a retirement plan, and savings equal to between three and six months' salary. Then, if you have twenty or more years to retirement, you can afford to become more aggressive, assuming higher risks and investing for growth.

As you enter your late forties and begin to prepare for retirement, you may want to switch to a mix of offensive and defensive investments. You have more to lose and less time to recover from losses.

Retirement brings the conservation years and a strategy that favors safe, high-yielding income investments. To combat inflation, mix these with blue-chip stocks or total-return mutual funds.

DIVERSITY

The navy never assigns all the sons and daughters of one family to the same ship. Not after the Sullivans lost all five sons when one ship went down. The same caution applies to investing. Put all your assets in one investment vehicle, and you could be sidelined or wiped out if it breaks down or is broadsided by the economy.

A balanced portfolio cuts your risks while speeding you toward your goals. How you divide your assets depends on the amount of money you have, your objectives, and your risk temperament.

You can diversify by having a mix of income-producing and growth-oriented investments. You can diversify further by combining intangible assets, such as stocks and bonds, with hard assets, such as real estate and gold. You can diversify by degree of risk, putting some cash into high-grade bonds and some into speculative issues.

For the busy investor, diversity is a two-edged sword. If you diversify too fully, you'll end up juggling more than you can handle. Tailor your strategy to include such investments as mutual funds, which let you put all your assets in one diversified basket. The extent to which a hands-off investor should diversify is discussed later.

PERIODIC REVIEW

Once you've decided on the route you want to take, don't waste time wandering off on every side road. Stick to your main highway. *Do* pull over at least once a year, though, to see if you've missed a turnoff or if there has been a change in road conditions. Adjust your strategy for economic downturns, changes in your financial situation, tax law revisions, and new investment opportunities.

CASTING INVESTMENTS IN THE RIGHT ROLES

Think of your portfolio as a theatrical road company, sent out to perform your financial plan. The actors are your investments. The roles they must play depend upon your financial goals. How well they perform depends upon how well they are cast.

You're the casting director. You must audition each investment before adding it to your portfolio. Fortunately each investment has its own character traits— bold, anxious, reckless, cautious, thrifty, profligate. Learn how to evaluate the role an investment is best suited to play, and your portfolio's performance will rate rave reviews.

Busy investors should give priority to investments with less dynamic personalities, ones that don't need constant attention. Rank other attributes according to how well they meet your needs.

Following are some of the general characteristics to analyze.

TIME INVOLVEMENT

How much management, monitoring, and misgivings go with the investment? Can you tuck it away without worry, or do you need to be chained to a ticker-tape machine? Can you check the price in the paper, or do you need a short-wave radio and homing pigeons? Can you peruse a slender prospectus, or do you need *Value Line*, economic data on five Latin countries, and global warming reports?

How can you tell if an investment is worry free? Time-efficient investments have certain traits in common, which we'll discuss in detail later in this chapter. They are

- Little research or training required
- Easy to invest or reinvest in
- Infrequent price swings
- Low risk
- Infrequent need to buy or sell
- Minimal diversification
- Simplified record keeping
- Meant to be held long-term
- Liquid or quickly sold
- No management required or professionally managed

Ten speedy investments are described in chapter 6. A chart rating investments by characteristic, with emphasis on time efficiency, can be found at the end of the chapter.

COST

Is an investment within your budget? Do you need $1,000 to join a money market fund or a sheik's ransom to move into a fixer-upper? Will investing a large percentage of your assets upset your efforts to diversify?

The initial investment may be only the beginning. Consider the effects of additional payments on your future cash flow. Does the investment produce income that can be used for paying expenses?

Be alert to false bargains. For example, low-priced or penny stocks are alluring because they are so cheap. For $3,000 you can get *3,000* shares of a stock priced at $1. But it's no easier for a $1 stock to go to $2 a share than it is for a stock to double from $50 to $100. Moreover, the dealer markups can be one-eighth of a point. That means you pay $1.125 for each share of $1 stock. The price must jump 12.5 percent before you break even. And a dip of only one-quarter point to $.75 reduces your investment by 25 percent ($1 minus $.25). Hardly a bargain.

INCOME

Does an investment supply a reliable stream of income? This is especially important to investors nearing retirement. Even if you plan to concentrate on growth, however, don't neglect the expected rate of return. If you're investing for the long term, a mere percentage point can mean thousands of dollars over time (see chapter 7).

Is your rate of return guaranteed? The amount of interest you receive on a certificate of deposit is fixed; the yield on a money market fund fluctuates with the market.

To counter the effects of inflation, look for an investment that yields at least 4 percent to 5 percent above the inflation rate (announced monthly in your daily paper). Remember, however, that the more attractive the yield, the greater the risk. Junk bonds, for example, pay a tempting 13 percent to 14 percent, but they are not secured by the companies that issue them. If the company fails, you'll lose your entire investment. Most income investments offer a minimum of fuss, an advantage for the time-conscious. Income investments include bonds, unit trusts, money market accounts, certificates of deposit, equity-income mutual funds, cash value annuities, utility stocks, and second trust deeds.

APPRECIATION

What's the investment's growth potential? Does it offer the possibility of a big price rise instead of a current income? The profit from appreciable assets, such as stocks, comes from a rise in value. By contrast, the value of cash investments never varies. The price of a share in a money market fund, for instance, is always $1. If an investment appreciates *and* pays income, so much the better. Dividend-paying stocks and rental real estate provide a mix of income and growth.

Perhaps no other investment can match the appreciation potential of your home. In the past twenty years home prices increased over 300 percent. Booming real estate markets have created a new class of the equity rich, who are cashing in on undreamed-of fortunes. Even with the current temporary slump in the housing market, buying your own home is still your smartest investment.

Appreciable assets generally demand more time to manage than investments that pay current income. To counteract fluctuating prices, diversify your holdings and monitor price swings as well as economic trends. On the other hand, growth investments should be held long-term, so little time is needed for selling and reinvestment. As a rule, these investments should be sold quickly only if 1. the price has plunged and holds no hope of recovery, or 2. the price has peaked.

Unlike fixed-income investments, appreciable assets

are inflation fighters. They tend to produce returns higher than the rate of inflation over the long term.

Growth investments include stocks, mutual funds, real estate, gold, silver, collectibles, and limited partnerships.

An excellent tool for increasing appreciation is leverage, discussed on pages 53–54. You can also help your capital grow by spending less on depreciable assets such as automobiles and furniture.

LIQUIDITY

Can you write a check to use your funds, or do you have to threaten someone to get them? The only way to get your money back from some limited partnerships is with a loaded gun. Money market funds, on the other hand, are completely liquid.

An investment is liquid if there's a ready market for it. One call to your broker is all that's needed to sell those shares of Technoco, for instance. However, such liquidity can be illusory. If Technoco is at an ebb, it's only liquid if you can accept a loss. IRA funds and certificates of deposit are also liquid—at a cost. Early withdrawal means a penalty. Real estate and collectibles are among the least liquid assets.

Analyze your short-term cash flow needs before investing in illiquid assets. How soon do you plan to have children, buy a home, start your own business? When and in what amounts will you need funds to meet your financial goals?

RISK

Is the investment safe? Is return of your principal guaranteed? The federal government guarantees Treasury bonds, bills, and notes. The Federal Deposit Insurance

Corporation (FDIC) insures bank accounts up to $100,000. Don't assume that all products offered by banks are guaranteed, however. Several of my clients lost thousands of dollars buying American Continental debentures from Lincoln Savings, believing that any losses would be federally insured. Had they asked, they would have learned that the debentures were merely unsecured obligations of American Continental, a shaky corporation that soon failed, paying its bond holders about fifteen cents on the dollar.

Guaranteed investments carry extremely low risk. The safety of nonguaranteed investments varies—from money market funds, in which no one has ever lost money, to stocks, which have tumbled as much as 43 percent in one year.

One sign of risk is volatility—that is, how much the price of an investment fluctuates. Cash investments, such as certificates of deposit and savings accounts, have zero volatility. Commodities are hair-raisingly volatile.

Volatile investments never give you any rest. Your waking hours will be spent glued to the telephone or to the financial news on CNBC. You'll have trouble concentrating, your digestion will suffer, and your nights will be sleepless. Volatile investments aren't for the busy investor.

Risks are not all of the Stephen King variety, however. All investments carry risk, even those that seem 100 percent safe. The culprit can be a stand-and-deliver highwayman, like market risk, or a sneak thief, like inflation. Altogether there are five broad categories of risk:

- **Market risk.** This is a term for such factors as Wall Street jitters and political crises that can buffet your investments. Tax law changes, program trading, trade agreements, and crowd psychology all contribute to market risk. The daily ups and downs of the stock market result from market risk. Gold and silver also carry considerable market risk, because their prices react gleefully to global strife and moodily to peace.

One common measure of market risk is the Standard & Poor's 500 Stock Index, published in the business section of most newspapers. You can compare the volatility of a stock against this index by referring to the *Value Line Investment Survey*, found in public libraries.

■ **Interest-rate risk.** This is the risk that rising interest rates will cause the value of an investment to drop. For instance, the price of existing bonds falls as rates go up, making their yields unattractive. Stocks of industries whose profits depend partly on interest rates, such as banks, savings and loans, and home builders, are also hostage to interest-rate risk. If you invest through a margin account or assume a variable-rate mortgage, you up your interest-rate risk, because higher borrowing costs reduce your profit.

■ **Inflation risk.** The relentless rise of prices erodes the purchasing power of an investment. Fifteen years of 5 percent inflation will reduce the value of $1,000 to $481. Low-yielding investments, such as savings accounts and certificates of deposit, may not earn enough to beat the climbing cost of living. Inflation also cuts the value of future income on fixed-income investments, such as long-term bonds.

Combat inflation by investing some of your money in inflation hedges, such as real estate, growth stock, and gold.

■ **Economic risk.** Slower economic growth can cause investments to fall in price. A drop in oil prices, for example, has already proven the economic risk of investing in Houston or Denver real estate. A recession can also hurt young growth companies and firms in cyclical industries, such as autos, transportation, and natural resources.

Recession-proof investments include long-term bonds and bond funds, zero-coupon bonds, money market funds, gold and gold funds, stocks of utilities, food retailers, and processors, and nondurable goods manufacturers.

- **Company-specific risks.** Stocks are vulnerable to events that affect only a particular company or industry. For example, the divorce of the company's founders clouded the future of Esprit. Investors also run a high degree of specific risk when they sink money into firms with heavy debt or limited partnerships run by inexperienced or dishonest general partners. Specific risk includes the chance a group of companies will be hurt by adverse government regulation.

The level of risk you choose should be influenced by your age, family situation, current and future earning power, net worth, tax bracket, and temperament. If you can tolerate risky investments, you'll be able to set aside less money to reach your goals, because the greater the risk, the greater potential return over time.

If you'd rather minimize investment risks, diversify among investments with varying degrees of risk.

LEVERAGE

Leveraging is the use of credit that lets you invest on borrowed funds. The less cash you put down, the greater the leverage. Mortgaged property and stock purchased on margin are the two most common leveraged investments.

Leverage dramatically increases the profit potential of

an investment. Suppose you buy a $150,000 house with no loan and sell it five years later for $187,500. The $37,500 gain is a 25 percent return on your investment. But if you'd invested only $30,000 of your own money and borrowed the other $120,000, you would have made $37,500 on a $30,000 investment. That's a 125 percent return.

The down side is that leverage can magnify losses. If you're forced to sell that $150,000 home for $135,000 instead, the $15,000 loss wipes out nearly half your $35,000—a 43 percent loss, even though the price of the property declined only 10 percent.

Leveraging is also expensive. An 11 percent mortgage equal to 90 percent of the purchase price of a house costs you $76,800 over five years. Most of that is interest, not buildup of equity, although it does have the saving grace of tax deductibility.

Leveraging is sound when you believe an asset will appreciate substantially or when inflation is high and your loan can be repaid in dollars that are steadily losing value.

Tax Impact

What are the tax benefits or burdens of the investment? If you're in a low tax bracket, you should be less concerned with taxes than with investing for the highest-possible yield. If you're trapped in the highest bracket, however, consider such tax-advantaged investments as rental real estate, which you can depreciate, or municipal bonds, which earn tax-exempt income.

There are three ways to minimize or avoid taxes.

1. You can earn tax-free income by

- investing in tax-exempt securities, such as municipal bonds or bond funds.

- investing in companies or mutual funds that pay dividends that are returns of capital or pass through tax-free interest.
- joining a firm that pays tax-free fringe benefits, such as health and life insurance.
- working overseas (up to $70,000 earnings tax free).
- selling your home for up to a $125,000 gain if you're age fifty-five or older.

2. You can defer income to lower-tax years by

- contributing to salary reduction [401(k)] plans.
- contributing to qualified retirement plans, such as IRAs, SEP-IRAs, and Keogh plans.
- investing in Series EE U.S. savings bonds.
- investing in whole-life, universal-life, and variable-life insurance and variable annuities.
- selling property on the installment basis.
- exchanging appreciated property for other property of a like kind.

3. You can create deductions by

- buying up to two personal residences.
- investing in commercial or residential real estate.
- investing in limited partnerships (losses are limited to income from similar activities).
- using a margin account to buy stock and writing off the interest expense.
- buying capital items, such as a computer or office furniture, for your self-employed business.
- incurring investment expenses, such as travel to inspect investment property and subscriptions to investment publications, books, and newsletters (subject to limitations based on your adjusted gross income).

Discuss tax considerations with your tax adviser as well as with the person selling the investment.

DIVERSIFICATION

Diversification is the shock absorber that insulates you from market ups and downs. By spreading your wealth among different investments, you limit the damage when one market hits a stretch of bad road.

Diversifying means assembling a risk-proof array of investments, from money market funds, stocks, and bonds to real estate and precious metals. The exact mix will be guided by your goals, how your assets are already invested, and your fondness for or aversion to risk. Don't get carried away and overdiversify, however, or you won't have time to manage your assets.

Take stock of your financial inventory first—not just the trophies you've collected in the stock market, but your cash, home equity, company pension plan, and the cash value of insurance policies. And don't overlook the biggest asset of all—your earning power. A salary of $50,000 a year is equal to the yield on a $500,000 portfolio invested at 10 percent. This means your finances are already heavily weighted toward risks that affect your profession. If you're a petroleum engineer, for example, you probably shouldn't buy oil stocks. By the same token, don't invest more than 10 percent of your assets in your company's stock.

Variety alone won't protect you, though, not if all your investments are vulnerable to the same risk. For example, you can own fifty stocks, but if they're in the airline, auto, rubber, steel, and textile industries, you're scarcely diversified. Those industries are all strongly affected by swings in the economy, so most will take a beating in a recession.

On the other hand, a portfolio of bonds and gold is

well diversified. Bonds generally go up as gold goes down and vice versa. But if you hold bonds and public utility stocks, both will decline when interest rates rise.

Once you decide on the right mix, resist the urge to move your money to investments that are temporarily performing better. A buy-and-hold strategy almost always triumphs. Adjust your portfolio about once a year to keep it balanced. For example, if an unprecedented bull market increases the value of your stock holdings, sell some of those shares and reinvest in asset categories that have lost ground.

THREE SAMPLE LAISSEZ-FAIRE PORTFOLIOS

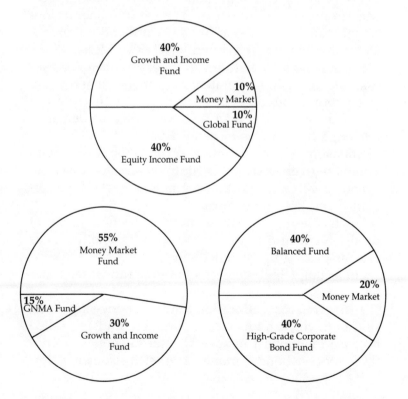

WALKING THE TIGHTROPE BETWEEN DIVERSITY AND TIME

Your goal as a harried investor is to build a portfolio that thrives under a variety of market conditions yet demands only occasional monitoring. But how much can you diversify before managing your investments demands too much of your time?

There are four basic ways you can diversify:

■ **Invest in mutual funds.** Most busy investors find that the best strategy is to take advantage of the abundance of stock, bond, and money market mutual funds. These funds spread your money among scores of securities in dozens of industries. You get full-time, professional management, sparing you work and research—all for a minimum investment of $1,000 or less.

Select at least three funds in different categories—for example, growth, corporate bonds, money market, and international. But don't buy into more than five funds if you're investing less than $100,000. The time demands outweigh the benefits of diversification.

Choosing a fund requires several hours' research. There are over 2,800 funds. But you shouldn't have to spend more than two hours a month tracking performance and keeping records.

For hassle-free investing, nothing beats a family of funds. Switching from one category to another is as easy as picking up the telephone.

For a complete discussion of mutual funds, see chapter 6.

■ **Invest in asset allocation funds.** For one-stop diversification, you can't top asset allocation funds, so-called because they invest in several asset categories at once (U.S. stocks, bonds, money market instruments, foreign securities, real estate, and metals). Thus, by choosing just one fund, you get instant diversification.

Asset allocation funds, therefore, eliminate almost all the research time required to choose your investments. However, you should still spend at least an hour a month reviewing the fund's performance and keeping records.

There are drawbacks. Some of these funds periodically rearrange their asset mix to benefit from short-term market fluctuations. This adds an element of fortune-telling and is at odds with the purpose of diversification. Moreover, most of these funds are new. Unless a fund has been around for at least five years and has a proven track record, don't rely on it as your only investment.

- **Hire a money manager.** You can turn over the controls entirely by hiring a money manager. He or she will decide how your investments should be diversified, manage your portfolio, and handle all the paperwork.

The time a money manager buys you doesn't come cheap. Annual fees start at 3 percent of your assets. What's more, most money managers are elitists, refusing to take on clients with assets of less than $100,000.

For information about selecting a money manager, see chapter 8.

- **Build your own portfolio.** This is by far the most time-consuming process. You should count on spending at least ten hours a week charting your investments and keeping up with news that could affect your holdings.

A diversified do-it-yourself portfolio requires at least $50,000. If you intend to buy individual securities, you'll need $15,000 for the stocks alone. For manageability, limit your holdings to between five and ten stocks spread among at least three industries, such as banking,

Investments at a Glance

Investment	Time Involvement	Inflation Hedge	Cost	Current Income	Appreciation Potential	Liquidity	Risk	Leverage	Tax Savings
EE savings bonds		○	○			◐		◐	●
Savings accounts		○	○	○		●			○
Money market mutual fund		◐	○	◐		●	○		
Bank money market		◐	>	◐		●	○		
Certificates of deposit	○	○	○	◐		◐			
U.S. Treasury issues									
Bills (1 year or less)	○	◐	●	◐	○	●	◐	◐	◐
Notes (1–10 yrs)	○	○	◐	◐	○	●	◐	◐	◐
Bonds (10–30 yrs)	○	○	◐	●	○	●	◐	◐	◐

Ginnie Mae cer-
tificates

Stock mutual
funds
Income
Growth

Blue-chip stocks

Zero-coupon
bonds
Treasury
Corporate

Single-premium
life (cash
value)

Annuities
Fixed
Variable

Land

Municipal bonds
(Long-term)

Corporate bonds
AAA grade
Junk

Investments at a Glance (continued)

Investment	Time Involvement	Inflation Hedge	Cost	Current Income	Appreciation Potential	Liquidity	Risk	Leverage	Tax Savings
Utility stocks	◐	◐	○	●	◐	●	◐	◐	
Gold	◐	●	○	○	●	●	●	●	
Common stocks	●	○	○	○	◐	●	●	◐	
Small-growth company	●	◐	○	○	●	◐	●	◐	
Preferred stocks	●	○	○	◐	◐	●	●	●	
Personal home	●	●	●		◐	○	◐	●	●
Commodities	●	●	○	◐	◐	●	●	●	○
REITs	●	●	○	●	●	●	●	◐	
Real estate limited partnerships	○	●	◐	◐	◐	○	●	●	◐
Oil and gas limited partnerships	○	●	◐	●	●	○	●	○	◐
Master limited partnerships	◐	●	◐	●	◐	●	●	◐	○

Coins
Fine art
Stock options
Second mort-
gages

KEY

● High
◑ Medium
○ Low
  Little or no degree
V Varies

Blank

electronics, and energy exploration. Studies show that putting equal amounts of money into five stocks eliminates 80 percent of the risk. Increasing your holdings to ten stocks wipes out 90 percent of the risk.

INVESTMENTS AT A GLANCE

You're too busy to test-drive every investment vehicle on the road. You need a quick way to sort the sedate from the sporty and to match the characteristics of particular investments to your financial goals. Then you can apply the principles you've learned in this chapter to design a portfolio that crosses your finish line first.

Use the preceding chart to narrow your choice of investments. Those requiring the least time are ranked first. Don't make that your sole criterion, however. Look for investments that combine time savings with most or all of the other characteristics you value.

Chapter 4

The Three-Step Financial Plan

I sense your impatience. You want to get on with the business of investing. After all, if you weren't in a hurry, you wouldn't have bought this book. And now I'm asking you to screech to a dead stop and come up with a financial plan, for Pete's sake.

I know it sounds dreary. The exciting world of accountancy is for bank managers who are too timid to become lion tamers, if I remember my Monty Python correctly. You don't want to fill out forms and worksheets. You want to climb right into the ring and waggle a chair at the Dreyfus lion, a bear market, or maybe even a TIGR or two.

Well, good for you. But before you dash off to join the investment circus, remember: you're investing on the run. And the less time you have to hit a target, the better your aim must be.

The target is where you want to be financially in ten, fifteen, twenty years. But this is a modern shooting gallery. The target's not moving, you are—between home, work, malls, and day care centers, in a round that would make a hummingbird dizzy. If you're going to shoot from the hip, at least make sure you can see the target clearly. At least have a financial plan.

Follow the steps outlined in this chapter, and you'll quickly have a target that's hard to miss. You'll also know the range and the right caliber of yield to hit your personal mark. You'll be ready to step out in the middle of Wall Street with your investment guns blazing.

GUESSING FOR SUCCESS—YOUR FINANCIAL PLAN

A financial plan is nothing more than a bull's-eye you can draw a rapid bead on. Put that plan in writing, however roughly, and even if your aim is hurried, your investments should hit dead center.

A financial plan can be as fancy as a rodeo rider's getup, but our sights are set on something more plain cowboy. We're not going to plot out your investing day to day to the grave. We're not going to weigh every investment with assay office precision to make sure your tax planning, insurance coverage, college savings, and estate planning are in perfect balance. Instead we're going to work through just three steps:

- Picking out your target (financial goal)
- Surveying your present position (net worth and cash flow)
- Estimating the necessary firepower (amount of savings needed to achieve your goals)

When we're through, you'll have a financial plan that's crude but safe enough for immediate investing. At some stage in your financial life, however, you should compute your cash flow and net worth in much finer detail. Consider hiring a financial planner or, if time no longer stalks you, consult one of the many financial planning books on the market.

Once you have your plan, stick by it. You don't want your target moving, too; that will only add to your ballistics problem. Fine-tune your plan, but don't change it unless your finances or goals alter substantially.

TARGET PRACTICE—SETTING GOALS AND PRIORITIES

What does success mean to you? One of my client couples is investing for the day they can volunteer to teach in Ecuador. Another wants to own a charter boat in Barbados. Still another hopes to build his computer store into a nationwide franchise.

Obviously your financial plan will be as unique as your thumbprint. There are no right or wrong goals, only ones that excite you because you believe in them. Don't set humdrum, Milquetoast goals; you'll be too bored to bother. Don't set goals within such easy reach that you can knock them off with a fly swatter. Give yourself a sense of adventure, a quest for the mountains of the moon, perhaps, or the silk route to China.

The goals you set shape your investment strategy. You're going to have the chance, here and now, to sort out your short- and long-term goals—in writing. If you're married, you and your spouse together should come up with your objectives. You may be surprised at how differently the two of you measure success in terms of money.

Here are a few guidelines:

- **Be creative.** Don't restrict yourself to bread-and-butter necessities. Toss in a treat or two.

- **Be specific.** Instead of "I want enough money to retire comfortably," write "I want my investments to earn at least $2,400 a month when I retire." Then you can compute exactly how much you need to save to meet your goal.
- **Attach a dollar amount to each of your goals.**
- **Set priorities.** Not every goal is equally important or achievable. Try classifying your objectives as "imperative," "needed, but not urgent," and "merely desirable." You may feel less like a boa faced with a cow to swallow.
- **Match your goals to your stage of life.** We all move through a financial life cycle. In our twenties a first home, building a career, and starting a family take priority. In our middle years college savings, acquiring a second home, and second careers hold our attention. Finally, retirement income, a retirement home, and estate planning become critical.

Pencils sharpened? Spend five minutes pinning down your short-term goals and ten minutes detailing your long-range ones.

GOALS AT A GLANCE

SHORT-TERM GOALS—Less than one year

Objective	Estimated cost	Date to achieve
Total cost		

LONG-TERM GOALS—More than one year

Objective	Estimated cost	Date to achieve

Total cost

GROWING WITH THE FLOW—IMPROVING YOUR CASH FLOW

Now that you know where your sights are set, it's time to take stock of your ammunition. Just how much money do you have left each year to invest toward your goals? This discretionary income is your cash flow, and you're about to find out how much you have by completing the Quick Income and Expense Worksheet.

Remember, we're not obsessed with working this out to the penny. Round figures may not please the IRS, but they're good enough here. Or you can compromise: add up your checks and credit card statements for the last three months and multiply by four. Do the same with your cash withdrawals, and allocate the total among the items you usually buy with cash.

Of course, if the exact amount can be figured fast, you may as well use it. Any fixed, periodic payments or receipts, such as your mortgage payment or paycheck, fall into this category. Another quick source: last year's tax return.

As a final measure, you might want to up expenses by 10 percent to 20 percent—the amount by which most people underestimate what they spend.

QUICK INCOME AND EXPENSE WORKSHEET

1. Annual income (salary, interest, dividends, rents, alimony, child support, pensions, Social Security)   _____
2. Annual income taxes (federal, FICA, state, local)   _____
3. After-tax income (line 1 minus line 2)   _____
4. Annual home expense (mortgage, rent, property tax, home insurance, utilities, repairs)   _____
5. Annual food and clothing   _____
6. Annual recreation/entertainment   _____
7. Annual car expenses   _____
8. Annual furnishings/appliances   _____
9. Annual medical and contributions   _____
10. Annual insurance premiums (health, life, disability)   _____
11. Annual child care/education   _____
12. Other   _____
13. Total annual living expenses (lines 4 through 12)   _____
14. Available for investment (line 3 minus line 13)   _____

MANAGING YOUR CASH FLOW

The amount on line 14 is your cash flow—that is, the difference between what comes in and what goes out each year. Your cash flow can be positive—or, if your finances resemble the sinking of the *Titanic,* negative. Obviously, if you consistently spend more than you make, you'll never have *any* money to save and invest. There are three ways to improve cash flow:

- Boost income
- Cut spending (budget)
- Borrow temporarily

We're going to focus on budgeting, because it's the most practical solution for the time-conscious money manager. You're too busy to boost income by taking a second job, and borrowing offers only short-term relief. In chapter 7 we'll discuss the power of savings and how it can save you time.

Your cash flow needs wise handling as well as control. The smart money manager follows these maxims:

- **Don't let cash sit idle.** You're working round the clock: why should your money be a freeloader? Give undeposited checks, uncashed traveler's checks, and large amounts of cash the boot at least once a week, and find them a job paying interest.
- **Don't prepay bills.** Oh, you can write the checks—in fact, the prompter the better. But drop them in your tickler file for mailing closer to the due date. Don't deprive your own funds of time, time spent earning interest.
- **Don't overwithhold taxes.** It's amazing how many coupon clippers and bargain hunters let the IRS borrow thousands of their dollars, not paying a nickel of interest, saying "If I had it, I'd spend it," or "I like a big refund, it pays for my vacation." Don't bank with the government. Claim the proper number of withholding allowances on your Form W-4.
- **Maximize savings.** There are many short-term parking places for money: checking accounts, passbook savings accounts, bank money markets, certificates of deposit, money market mutual funds, U.S. savings bonds. Frankly I'd put most of it in the one paying the highest interest.

YOUR FIRING RANGE—COMPUTING YOUR NET WORTH

Your distance from your goals determines your choice of investment weapons. You can't hit a target miles away with a derringer. You'll need one of finance's big guns—usually aggressive and riskier investments. Less firepower is needed for medium-range objectives—moderate-risk Colts and Winchesters, such as growth stock mutual funds and residential rental units.

How far away is your target? You need to compute two numbers—the dollar figure where you stand (your current net worth) and the dollar figure at the site of your target (desired net worth). Measure the difference, and you have your range.

Net worth is simply the difference between what you own and what you owe. If you were to cash out today—sell everything and pay off all your debts—net worth is how much would be left over.

Take the next fifteen minutes or so to fill in the Quick Net Worth Worksheet. It may look like a lot of work, but remember, you don't have to be precise. Be exact only if the information is easy to obtain. For cash assets, refer to your latest bank, brokerage, or mutual fund statements. For securities, check your newspaper for price quotes.

Cash, bank and money market accounts, and marketable securities are liquid assets—that is, they can be converted quickly to folding money. Generally, between 15 percent and 20 percent of your assets should be liquid, and there should be enough ready cash to cover three to six months' of expenses.

Illiquid assets are harder to value. Your home and other real estate should be listed at current market value. Use the recent sales price of another neighborhood property, if known. Or increase your purchase price by an assumed inflation rate of 6 percent for every year you've owned the property.

The tables in your life insurance policies or annuities show their current cash values. The value you place on your personal property will be a guess. Be conservative: if you had to sell quickly, you'd probably get only a fraction of what they're worth. If you find you're completely stumped, put down your cost.

As for debts, check last year's year-end mortgage statement (Form 1098) for the outstanding balance. Tally up the unpaid bills sitting on your desk. Drag out last year's tax return and estimate the probable damage this year—higher if you're making more, lower if your income is down or your deductible expenses are up.

Now subtract your liabilities from your assets. If you come up with a negative figure, drop a lifeboat. Seriously, I think you'll be surprised at how much you're actually worth. Brag all you want.

If you're enjoying this, you might want to go one or two steps further and compute your current ratio and your debt-to-equity ratio. Your current ratio is figured by dividing your total assets by your total liabilities. If, for example, you come up with 3.2, it means you have more than three times the assets needed to meet your current debts.

Your debt-to-equity ratio is used by banks to decide if you're creditworthy. Low ratios make bankers jovial. Don't go overboard, though. Too low a debt ratio may mean your investments aren't working hard enough for you. Compute your debt-to-equity ratio by dividing your total liabilities by your net worth.

Your net worth is your working capital. It's the point from which you fire at your target.

TAX PLANNING

Reduce the tax bite, and your net worth shoots up much faster. We've all heard about the magic of tax-free investing: how $2,000 invested annually over thirty years in a tax-deferred IRA earns four times as much as the same amount sunk in a taxable investment.

Well, it's true. In mapping out your investment strategy, don't disdain to take advantage of the options Congress has grudgingly granted to defer income—IRAs, SEP-IRAs, Keoghs, or employer-sponsored 401(k) or 403(b) plans.

QUICK NET WORTH WORKSHEET

1. Cash and cash equivalent assets (bank accounts, money market accounts, CDs, T-bills, employee savings plans) _____
2. Stocks, bonds, and mutual funds _____
3. Total liquid assets (line 1 plus line 2) _____
4. Retirement funds (IRAs, Keoghs, 401(k) plans, and other company plans) _____
5. Real estate (value of your home, second home, rental property, land, limited partnerships) _____
6. Cash value of life insurance and annuities _____
7. Collectibles (art, antiques, stamps, precious metals) _____
8. Personal property (cars, furniture, jewelry) _____
9. Total assets (lines 3 through 8) _____
10. Unpaid bills (mortgage or rent, income/property taxes, alimony/child support, medical) _____
11. Credit card/charge account balances _____

12. Loans (mortgages, home equity, car,
     education, margin account)   _____
13. Total liabilities (lines 10 through 12)   _____
14. Net worth (line 9 minus line 13)   _____

HOW TO GET FROM WHERE YOU ARE TO WHERE YOU WANT TO BE

Roll out the time machine, we're going back to your future, back to the goals you set at the beginning of this chapter—and your estimated cost of those wishful objectives. Now it's time to find out how much you must set aside today to realize your dreams tomorrow.

From the worksheet above, you have an idea of your current net worth. Your desired net worth is the total of all the price tags you've attached to your dreams. Bridging this gap between the present and the future should be the driving force behind the investment strategy you develop in chapter 5.

Because we're traveling into the future, our math begins to resemble some of Doc Brown's blackboard hieroglyphics. The $3,218 you deposit today at 8 percent will be worth $15,000 in twenty years. This is an illustration of the time value of money, discussed in chapter 7.

Another time warp is inflation. For every dollar deposited by the passage of time, at least a nickel is being eroded away by inflation. Both of these factors—interest or dividends building up your net worth, inflation tearing it down—must figure in your calculations. Inflation of 4 percent a year will stunt the growth of the $3,218 you deposited above at 8 percent, giving your $15,000 a purchasing power of only $7,051 in twenty years.

The other variables in your equation are the date you're headed for in the future and the rate of return on your investments.

A financial calculator will whisk you to October 25, 2015, or wherever else you're going, in the least time. If you don't own one of these wizards, however, you're welcome to use my battered DeLorean, the Bridging the Gap Worksheet.

BRIDGING THE GAP WORKSHEET

1. Current net worth (from Quick Net Worth Worksheet)   _____

2. Desired net worth   _____

3. The gap (line 1 minus line 2)   _____

4. Number of years available   _____

5. Amount needed after inflation (line 3 times appropriate factor from the following table)   _____

YEARS AVAILABLE

5	1.28*
10	1.63
15	2.08
20	2.65
25	3.39
30	4.32

*5% annual inflation assumed

6. Future value of your current net worth (line 1 times appropriate factor from the following table)   _____

Years Available	Rate of Return		
	10%	15%	20%
5	1.61	2.01	2.49
10	2.60	4.05	6.19
15	4.18	8.14	15.41
20	6.73	16.37	38.34
25	10.83	32.92	95.40
30	17.45	66.21	237.38

7. Total needed to achieve desired net
   worth (line 5 minus line 6) _____

8. Monthly savings required (line 7 times
   appropriate factor from following
   table) _____

Years Available	Rate of Return		
	10%	15%	20%
5	.013	.011	.010
10	.005	.004	.003
15	.002	.001	.0009
20	.001	.0007	.0003
25	.0008	.0003	.0001
30	.0004	.0001	.00004

Return now to your Quick Income and Expense
Worksheet. How does your actual amount of cash available for investment compare with the ideal amount here
on line 8? If line 8 is too much to manage, repeat the
computation using a higher rate of return. Remember,
though, that higher yield means higher risk (see Table
of Investment Yields, page 78). If you don't want to take
on extra risk, budgeting may be necessary to increase
your savings.

Of course, it's possible your current net worth needs

time to grow or your goals exceed your means. In that case you'll have to set your sights lower until your net worth increases.

TABLE OF INVESTMENT YIELDS

5% to 10%	10% to 15%	15% to 20%
Savings accounts	High-yield	Options
CDs	bond funds	Initial public
Money market	High-yield	offerings
investments	stocks	Aggressive
EE savings	Growth stocks	growth funds
bonds	Growth and in-	Junk bonds
Treasury	come funds	Growth-oriented
securities	Real estate	limited part-
High-grade	(direct	nerships
bond funds	ownership)	
Annuities	Income-oriented	
Municipal bonds	limited part-	
	nerships	

With the knowledge of how much to save and the yield needed to bridge the gap, your financial planning ends. You have a "can't miss" target, you've counted your bullets, and you've computed your range. You're ready to start investing as soon as you pick your weapons. In the next chapter you'll learn what factors to consider before you make your selection.

Chapter 5

Ten Timeless Investment Strategies

The leisurely investor is like a gourmet: he has time to select the choicest investment vehicles, time to mix them painstakingly, time to stir them endlessly, time to savor the results.

For the busy investor, however, investing must be as quick, convenient, and functional as microwave cooking. The following techniques are to saving and investing what TV dinners are to haute cuisine.

AUTOMATIC PAYROLL DEDUCTION PLANS

These plans make saving as effortless as breathing. Part of your paycheck is spirited away before you ever lay eyes on it and invested in your choice of an IRA, money market fund, savings account, or EE savings bonds. You decide the amount and how often you want it deducted. Interest is modest, but you can't even stuff cash under your mattress this fast.

If your employer doesn't offer such a program, banks

and credit unions do. Take a few minutes to fill out an authorization form, and the bank will deduct a set amount from your checking account on a day you name, such as the first of the month. Banks also automatically transfer funds from a checking into a money market or savings account. Some banks allow transfers to a mutual fund, usually without charge.

If you belong to a credit union at work, a portion of your paycheck can be deposited automatically into your share account.

(401)K PLANS

If your employer offers a 401(k) plan, pump every nickel you can into it. Why? Under a 401(k) plan, the portion of your pay that you decide to tuck away is treated as unearned until you retire. That means your contribution is currently nontaxable. It doesn't even show up as part of wages on your Form W-2. Second, your earnings compound tax-deferred. This double indemnity from taxes can make you wealthy indeed.

Let's look at $4,000 invested with and without a 401(k) shelter. You'll have $1,450 more after one year with a 401(k) plan, or a return of 36 percent more on your original investment.

One-Year Growth Comparison

	With 401 (k)	Without 401 (k)
Amount invested	$4,000	$4,000
Taxes (top rate 31%)	(0)	(1,240)
Net investment	$4,000	$2,760
Earnings, 1 year (10%)	400	276
Tax on earnings (31%)	(0)	(86)
Account balance after one year	$4,400	$2,950

Multiply the result by twenty-five years, and you'll see how a moderate 401(k) investment could comfort you with a six-figure retirement fund.

The prospects are even more delightful if your employer matches 25 percent to 100 percent of your contribution. In that case your nest egg appreciates 25 percent to 100 percent before it's even invested.

Let's assume your employer puts in 50 percent of the $4,000 you contribute in our example above, or $2,000. After one year your account now grows to $6,600—$3,650 more than in a taxable account and 91 percent more on your original investment. In ten years your account with be worth $127,268.

The maximum you may contribute is $8,728 a year (indexed for inflation). Matching contributions by your employer may bring the total to $30,000 or 25 percent of your salary, whichever is lower.

You don't have to contribute the maximum amount, but you may be surprised at how small a bite a 401(k) takes out of your paycheck. Because your contribution reduces your salary and puts you in a lower tax bracket, less federal, state, and local income taxes are withheld (Social Security withholding—as unstoppable as the Terminator—goes on). In many cases this drop in withholding almost equals your contribution. The result: a net paycheck that lets you pocket almost as much as when you weren't investing a dime.

Note: Because a 401(k) reduces your salary, you may not want to contribute if you're nearing retirement and your company pension benefits are based on your last three to five years' salary.

A 401(k) doesn't keep you from having a Keogh or a deductible IRA (if your adjusted gross income is less than $35,000 single or $50,000 joint—if your income is higher, your IRA contribution cannot be deducted). If your resources are limited, however, take full advantage of the 401(k) before contributing to the others, because of its superior compounding power.

You'll be offered three or more investment options. Common choices include stock funds, bond funds, money market funds, guaranteed investment contracts (sponsored by insurance companies), and your employer's stock. As a general rule, no more than 10 percent of your retirement savings should be invested in your company's stock. (Your company will probably make its matching contributions in shares.)

Most companies allow you to change your options quarterly or semiannually. In the case of mutual funds, you may often switch from one type of fund to another daily.

Choose an investment mix appropriate for your age and financial goals. Unless you're close to retirement, don't be overly cautious. For example, according to a survey by Hewitt Associates, an employee benefits consulting firm, guaranteed investment contracts (GICs) are by far the most popular investment choice, receiving 64 percent of plan contributions. Although these insurance-backed investments are considered safe, GICs yield only slightly more than money market funds or Treasury securities. They may not be the best choice for young investors, therefore, whose biggest risk is generally inflation.

Consider your 401(k) in light of your other investments. If all your non–401(k) money is in Treasury bills, for instance, you might want to invest a higher percentage of your 401(k) in stocks.

Because 401(k)s are tax-deferred, invest in options such as mutual funds or fixed-income investments that normally bear a heavy tax. For the same reason, avoid high-risk investments—any losses you suffer won't be deductible.

Before investing, ask the plan administrator for information on the performance of the plan's investments. Compare the one-year and five-year rates of return with averages for similar investments.

Note: Nonprofit organizations offer a 403(b) plan. This plan is just like a 401(k), with one major exception: a 403(b) plan requires you to invest your funds in an annuity account through an insurance company. You may not invest in stocks and mutual funds.

One caveat: A 401(k) is nearly as untouchable as Eliot Ness. This is a retirement savings plan, after all. You may not withdraw funds until you reach age 59½, or you'll be slapped with a 10 percent penalty. The only exceptions are if you leave the company, become disabled, or suffer economic hardship. Hardship generally means uninsured medical or accident expenses, the threat of foreclosure or eviction, or the need for a down payment on your home or to pay college costs. However, even if your situation qualifies as a hardship, you must first exhaust other means of raising the money, including borrowing from your 401(k) account.

Actually a 401(k) loan has one unique advantage—the interest you pay goes back into your account. The down side is that your money is no longer earning interest tax free.

You can borrow half your vested balance, up to $50,000. The loan must be paid back within five years, unless you're using the money to buy your home. Then you have up to thirty years to repay, through payroll deductions.

Tax on a withdrawal can be deferred by rolling it over into an IRA account within sixty days. If you switch jobs, you may also postpone the tax by rolling over your money (including any outstanding loan balance) into your new employer's 401(k) plan.

COMPANY PROFIT-SHARING PLANS

If investing so much time at the office leaves you no time to invest, take advantage of your company's own pension or profit-sharing plan, if available. After all, your efforts contribute to the profits. Why shouldn't your time investment pay as well as an investment of money?

Company plans vary widely, but all offer a fast and easy way to invest for retirement. Ask your personnel office for details.

The size of your employer's contribution depends on company profits. A few profitable companies distribute a portion of their earnings to employees periodically as a bonus. Invest any profits you receive directly in one of the ten speedy investments recommended in chapter 6.

Most companies hold your share of the profits in a trust. If that is the case, you won't have to make even an elementary investment decision.

In addition to the company's contribution, many profit-sharing plans allow you to make voluntary contributions under a 401(k) option. These are often matched by your employer, and earnings are tax-deferred. Don't sign up, however, until you know

- how well the plan or trust has performed.
- how much you can put in each year.
- how much the company matches.
- what restrictions there are on withdrawals.

A key advantage of these plans is that they are tax-deferred—that is, you pay no income taxes until you withdraw your share of the profits from the pool.

No matter how convinced you are that your company is the next IBM (or even if it *is* IBM), never place all your investment bets there: guard against your company falling on hard times by diversifying.

COMPANY SAVINGS OR THRIFT PLANS

With these retirement plans, you authorize your employer to invest a part of your salary through automatic payroll deductions. The most common contribution is 3 percent to 6 percent of your annual salary. The big bonus: your employer usually matches all or part of your contribution. Most employers chip in fifty cents, but one in five companies will match you dollar for dollar.

Nearly nine out of ten savings plans have a 401(k) feature, which means some of the money you sock away reduces the amount of your taxable salary.

Need more convincing? You pay no tax on your employer's contribution until you take it out at retirement or leave the company. And all dividends, interest, and capital gains your savings earn are also tax-deferred.

Contributions to a savings plan go into an employee trust fund. As a rule, your company lets you direct where your own assets are invested. You usually have two to three options of varying risks. Slightly more than half of all companies give you a say about where to invest their matching contributions. The others are less democratic—company contributions go into company stock.

There are two drawbacks. First, many plans have vesting provisions that range from two to six years. If you leave the company before becoming vested, you forfeit your employer's matching contribution. Second, you face a 10 percent penalty on any money withdrawn before age 59½, unless you're disabled or will suffer financial hardship. This penalty can be avoided by rolling your savings over into an IRA within sixty days.

Each company plan has different restrictions. Ask how much you may invest, the amount your employer will match, whether you must be vested to tap your savings, and the tax consequences.

EMPLOYEE STOCK PURCHASE PLANS (ESOPs)

There's one stock you don't have to research—your employer's. Companies often let employees buy stock at bargain prices. Over the years the rewards can be staggering.

The amount you decide to invest is deducted automatically from your paycheck. Most companies require you to contribute at least 1 percent of your salary to the plan. Your employer usually picks up the tab for any commissions or administrative expenses. The company saves you still more time by doing all the record keeping.

You're not taxed on any gain or loss until you sell the stock. There's no penalty for withdrawing dividends the plan earns.

Most ESOPs don't permit you to borrow against your account or to take out cash until you retire or quit. Ask your personnel department about vesting requirements. Because their purpose is to boost productivity and morale, ESOPs tend to vest more rapidly than other benefit plans.

DOLLAR-COST AVERAGING

Don't waste time waiting for the perfect moment to jump in and buy stock. Use a simple investing technique called dollar-cost averaging. You invest a fixed amount, say, $100, every month, whether the price of the shares you're buying is going down or up.

What's the benefit? Over the long term—five or ten years—you're likely to acquire more shares at median, rather than high, prices.

For example, suppose you invest $300 in May to buy ten shares at $30 per share. In June the price drops, and your $300 buys twenty shares at $15 per share. You end up with thirty shares at an average price of $20.

The discipline of this installment plan approach keeps you from making two common mistakes: investing all your money when prices are high and selling out at a big loss when prices are depressed.

Best of all, dollar-cost averaging takes almost no time at all. Simply arrange an automatic transfer between your bank and a mutual fund. Or authorize payroll deductions. The same amount of money will be withdrawn on a specified date every month and transferred to the fund of your choice. Fine-tune the amount you're investing at least annually, however, to adjust for salary increases and inflation.

Although you can dollar-cost average with any amount, it's not economical to purchase individual stocks this way, because the commission on a small order takes too big a bite out of profits. The commission is even costlier for trading odd lots (under one hundred shares) of stock. That's why dollar-cost averaging works best with mutual funds, preferably those with no load (sales charge).

One way to use dollar-cost averaging without going through a broker is to buy shares in a company that has a dividend reinvestment plan (see page 88).

If you have a lump sum to invest, such as a pension plan distribution or an inheritance, you can dollar-cost average by investing part of the money in regular installments. Bank the uninvested portion in a money market account.

IRA investors can set aside $165 a month, rather than waiting until the approach of April 15 to rustle up $2,000.

If dollar-cost averaging becomes too boring for you, experiment. For instance, increase the level of your investment as share prices fall, and decrease it as prices rise. To do this, you have to keep a record of the average cost of your investments. When the share price of your fund rises above your average cost, invest less; when it dips below, invest more.

To find out how much to invest, divide your average cost by the fund's current price, and multiply that figure by the amount of your regular contribution. For example, suppose you've been investing $100 monthly. If your average cost is $9 and the market price is now $10, decrease your investment to $90 ($\frac{9}{10} \times \$100$).

Another variation is to use more than one fund. In a bull market, invest your fixed amount in an aggressive growth fund. Switch to a growth and income fund in uncertain periods. And head for a straight income fund if the stock and bond markets take a prolonged downturn. A family of funds is handiest for pursuing this strategy.

DIVIDEND REINVESTMENT PLANS (DRPs)

One of the laziest ways to build a portfolio is through automatic dividend reinvestment. About 1,000 companies let you invest your quarterly dividends in additional shares, usually without levying a broker's commissions. About 170 companies even offer 3 percent to 5 percent discounts.

Many companies also let you buy still more shares by investing another $10 to $5,000 on top of your reinvested dividend, again bypassing a broker. All your money goes toward the purchase of shares, none for expenses. Mail your cash contribution close to the monthly or quarterly payment date to avoid losing too much interest.

To participate you must own a company's stock, although the number of shares varies. In some plans one share is enough; others require fifty or one hundred. Don't sign on unless you plan to hold the shares long-term.

The benefits of dividend reinvestment are indisputable. DRPs offer

- a way to invest small amounts at substantial savings in broker's fees and administrative costs without lifting a finger.
- forced savings of small cash dividends that might otherwise be frittered away.
- a compounding effect from periodic reinvesting that magically increases the value of your investments.
- the advantage of dollar-cost averaging in avoiding peak buying.
- the opportunity to build a diversified portfolio of America's leading companies for a modest initial investment.

Reinvested dividends are taxable, just as if you received them in cash. Tax is based on the fair market value of the stock on the dividend payment date.

Note: Keep *every* cumulative year-end statement you receive under this plan. You'll need them to determine your basis in the stock when you sell it.

You can obtain a list of companies offering dividend reinvestment plans by sending $2 to Public Relations Dept., Standard & Poor's Corp., 25 Broadway, New York, NY 10004.

ASSET MANAGEMENT ACCOUNTS (AMAs)

An asset management account does everything but walk your dog. These all-in-one accounts are terrific time-saving, money-management tools, because they consolidate your record keeping and provide nearly every type of financial service under one roof. Bearing brand names, such as Merrill Lynch CMA and Schwab One, they combine a brokerage margin account with a money market account, a checking account, and a credit card. To top it all off, they track all your banking and securities transactions on a single statement.

Most asset management accounts offer free checking. Unlike money market funds, AMAs usually require no minimum check size and place no limit on the number of checks you may write. Most AMAs come with a debit or charge card to make purchases or withdraw cash at banks and ATMs worldwide. With these cards, your purchases are paid off automatically using money in your account. If your spending exceeds your funds, no problem. Your debit card also provides a line of credit. The amount you can borrow depends upon the market value of your securities.

Some accounts issue true credit cards that let you finance purchases. The amount you borrow comes from a bank, not the brokerage firm, and you pay high bank card rates on your unpaid balance.

For a few dollars more, you can deposit your paychecks into your AMA and have your fixed, monthly bills paid automatically. Every transaction is shown on your monthly statement, or you can call toll-free, twenty-four hours a day, to check on your balance and lines of credit.

You can choose from taxable or tax-free funds and, in some cases, federally insured money market accounts. Deposits or withdrawals from these funds incur no sales commission. Dividends, interest, deposits, and proceeds from the sale of stock are automatically invested daily or weekly into the money fund of your choice. The interest rates paid by AMAs are generally higher than those paid by bank checking accounts.

One of the prime benefits of asset management accounts becomes apparent at tax time. They provide a year-end summary of your investment income and securities transactions. The most comprehensive include summaries of your deductible expenses and capital gains and losses as well.

In choosing an AMA, ask the following:

- **What's the minimum deposit?** Generally these accounts are a high-stakes game. Minimum deposit requirements usually range from $5,000 to $25,000 in cash or marginable securities (that is, listed stock, many over-the-counter stocks, mutual funds, and corporate or government bonds). AMAs with low deposit requirements include the Consolidated Asset Management (CAM) with no minimum deposit, Quick & Reilly ($500), and Edward D. Jones's Full Service account ($1,000).
- **What's the minimum balance?** There's usually no requirement that a large sum be kept in the account once it's opened. Many accounts have no minimum balance requirement at all. Others, such as those at Citibank, require you to supply more funds or close the account if your balance falls below $10,000.
- **Do I get a debit card or a credit card?** A debit card, with its substantially lower interest rate, is more desirable.
- **What's the annual fee?** These range from no fee (CAM, Schwab One, IDS Financial) all the way up to $100 (Citibank, Paine Webber).
- **How has the AMA's mutual fund performed over the past year? Five years? How does that stack up against regular mutual funds?**
- **How often is my account swept into a money market fund?** Oppenheimer Executive Assets Account, for example, sweeps amounts under $10,000 weekly instead of daily. This can cost you interest, although the amount lost on a typical $500 balance would be minimal.

- **What's the ATM transaction fee?** Many AMAs levy a hefty $1 per transaction. Smith Barney charges 1.5 percent of the amount withdrawn, or a minimum of $2.
  - **Are canceled checks returned?** If so, is there a fee?
  - **How do I intend to use the account?** Do you want it mainly for money management? If so, you may have to choose a high-fee, high-balance account. No-fee, low-balance accounts, such as Schwab One, welcome only investors who want to trade actively in securities.

AMAs do have some drawbacks. For one thing, an AMA is as close to a personal financial valet as you can get. It's a luxury to park your assets in one spot and be relieved of all money management chores. Dangerously so. While you're loafing, your broker will be investing all your assets in your brokerage firm's mutual funds or in stocks or limited partnerships your broker makes a market in. Pretty soon you won't be diversified anymore. And the track record of most brokerage firms' mutual funds, especially, has been mediocre at best. Store only enough cash in an AMA to meet your checking needs. Resist the AMA's invitation to abdicate and hand it the throne.

AMAs may also be a trap for the unwary, because most are margin accounts—your broker automatically extends you credit using your stocks, mutual funds, or bonds as collateral. Unless you monitor your statements closely, you might not even realize you've borrowed money.

Worse, you receive no regular monthly bill. The loan balance can remain unpaid indefinitely. You must discipline yourself to pay off the debt. Until you do, interest keeps mounting, although rates are reasonable—.75 percent to 2.25 percent above the prime rate. Moreover, because you can't borrow more than 50 percent of your securities' value, a decline in market value may trigger a margin call if you've borrowed heavily. This means you must add more cash or stock to your AMA to bring your equity up to the 50 percent margin requirement. If you don't meet this call, your securities will be sold by your broker.

You can avoid the pitfalls of a margin account by opening a cash-only account, which doesn't offer a credit line. But then, of course, you give up overdraft protection.

FORMULA INVESTING

If your schedule didn't already resemble the invasion of Normandy, you could bury yourself in charts—tracking trading volume, moving averages, and Dow Jones industrials. You could spot trends and turning points, rallies and slumps. As it is, you have about as much time to manage stock holdings as you do to watch grass grow.

Don't let that keep you out of the stock market, though. You can build a portfolio that won't go down in flames without your constant attention. The secret is formula investing, designed to neutralize market swings.

Formula (or ratio) investing spreads your buying and selling over the ups and down of the market. It ignores short-term swings and demands patience and self-discipline. If you adopt this technique, stick to it. Follow it consistently in spite of hunches, insider tips, and alarming headlines.

Some paperwork is inevitable: you must keep track of your total returns.

Formula investing can be used with stock mutual funds as well as with individual stocks. Following are two viable formula plans.

A QUICK GUIDE TO ASSET MANAGEMENT ACCOUNTS

Account	Minimum to open	Minimum balance	Annual fee	Card	Bill paying
A. G. Edwards & Sons Total Asset Account 800-325-8380	$20,000	None	$ 50	Debit	No
Charles Schwab Schwab One 800-421-4488	5,000	None	0	Debit	No
Citibank Focus 800-752-0800	25,000	10,000	100	Debit	
Consolidated Asset Management CAM 800-423-2345	Any	None	0	None	
Dean Witter Reynolds Active Assets Account 800-231-0505	10,000	None	80	Debit	Yes
E. F. Hutton Asset Management Account 800-325-0038	10,000	5,000	100	Credit	
Fidelity Investments Fidelity USA Ultra Service Account 800-544-6262	25,000	1,000	60	Credit	Yes

A QUICK GUIDE TO ASSET MANAGEMENT
ACCOUNTS (*continued*).

Account	Minimum to open	Minimum balance	Annual fee	Card	Bill paying
Kemper Money Plus 800-621-1048	5,000	None	65	Debit	
IDS Financial IDS Cash Management 800-328-8300	2,000	300	0	None	
Merrill Lynch Cash Management Account 800-262-4636	20,000	None	80	Debit	Yes
Oppenheimer Executive Assets Account 800-327-8324	20,000		100	Credit	No
Paine Webber Resource Mgmt. 800-937-7071	15,000	10,000	100	Credit	
Prudential Bache Command Account 800-222-4321	15,000	None	75	Debit	Yes
Quick & Reilly Cash Management Service 800-926-0600	500		0	None	No

A QUICK GUIDE TO ASSET MANAGEMENT
ACCOUNTS (*continued*)

Account	Minimum to open	Minimum balance	Annual fee	Card	Bill paying
Shearson Lehman Financial Management Account 800-221-3636	10,000	5,000	50	Credit	No
Smith Barney, Harris Upham Vantage 800-225-1508	10,000	None	40	Credit	No

CONSTANT DOLLAR RATIO PLAN

Under this plan, you decide upon a certain dollar value for your holdings. If a stock rises, you take the profit, then invest in another stock or buy shares of the same stock when the value goes down. If the price falls, you buy more at the lower price to bring your investment back up to the specified dollar amount.

For example, suppose you decide to maintain $10,000 worth of a growth stock. If your investment appreciates to $12,000 in a given time period, say, six months, you'd sell $2,000 worth. If the value of the shares falls to $9,000, you'd buy $1,000 worth to restore your holdings to the $10,000 level.

CONSTANT RATIO PLAN

This strategy blends dollar-cost averaging (see page 86) with a formula for adjusting the mix of investments in your portfolio.

First, divide your investments between stocks and more conservative assets, depending on the amount of risk you're willing to take. Conservative investors might want to split their money evenly between a stock fund and a money market fund.

Begin by making equal monthly contributions to each fund—for example, $100 to the stock fund and $100 to the money fund. Now monitor your portfolio values. If a move in stock prices makes the stock fund worth considerably more or less than the money fund, shift assets to make them equal again.

Let's take an example. You have $5,000 invested in a global fund and $5,000 in a money market, and you want to keep this constant fifty-fifty ratio. Your plan calls for adjustment whenever the shares in either fund exceed 55 percent of the total value of the portfolio. If the value of the global fund edges up to $5,500, you'll transfer $500 from the stock fund to the money market to maintain your ratio. But if the global fund sinks to $4,500—buoying the money market to 55 percent— you'll move $500 in the opposite direction, from the money market to the stock fund. The size of your monthly contribution remains unchanged.

Generally, 5 percent is the maximum divergence you should use as a trigger, or you'll rarely make an adjustment.

PREPAY YOUR MORTGAGE

The stonemasons who built Notre Dame had to wait a lifetime to see the result of their handiwork, but when they did their reward was stupendous. On a less spiritual plane, you can be similarly gratified by prepaying your mortgage.

Your time saving won't come for ten, fifteen, or twenty-two years. That's when the mortgage is finally burned and you never have to make the monthly payment again. But you're building a cathedral, remember. And the truly breathtaking saving is that of mortgage interest.

You've heard about the power of compound interest (if not, see chapter 7). It pumps up your savings like steroids as time goes by. Unfortunately, a mortgage wields this power in reverse. Take out a $120,000 mortgage at 10 percent over thirty years, and you'll pay back $379,476. That's the original $120,000 you borrowed, plus *$259,276* in interest.

Barely 5 percent of your payments in the first year on a thirty-year loan go to principal. Even by the end of the tenth year, less than 13 percent of your payment reduces principal. It takes twenty-three years before your monthly payment splits fifty-fifty between principal and interest.

On our $120,000 mortgage at 10 percent, adding an extra $25 a month for principal to the regular payment of $1054.10 shortens the mortgage from thirty to twenty-six years and slashes $37,402 off the interest.

How does prepaying work this miracle? Take a look at this amortization table for a thirty-year $75,000 loan at 10 percent with a monthly payment of $658.18:

Monthly Payment	Interest	Principal	Balance
1	$625.00	$33.18	$74,966.82
2	624.72	33.46	74,933.36
3	624.44	33.74	74,899.62
4	624.14	34.02	74,865.60
5	623.88	34.30	74,831.30
6	623.59	34.59	74,796.71

Reducing the principal balance at this rate is like trying to save up $75,000 by dropping pennies in your piggy bank.

But if you add $33.46 to your first payment (the second month's principal), your lender skips the second line entirely. The $624.72 interest normally charged against payment number two is never charged, and you've shortened your mortgage by one month.

Do this three times and you'll save over $1,800 in interest and take three months off the life of your loan.

Remember: Prepayments are not an extra cost. They're amounts you'd be writing checks for anyway if you hadn't taken this (eventual) time-saving measure.

There are at least seven prepayment strategies, but only the two fastest are discussed here:

■ **Make flat-sum payments.** Think of your monthly mortgage payment as being $25, $50, $100, or $150 higher each month than it actually is. Choose an amount that won't strain your finances.

The flat-sum method saves you from having to take time to find out the next month's principal and adding that precise amount to your check.

Here's how this method affects a $100,000, 10.5 percent, thirty-year mortgage:

| Flat Sum Payoff | | |
Per Month	In Years	Interest Saved
$ 25	25.6	$40,783
$ 50	22.7	$66,309
$100	19.0	$98,377
$150	16.5	$118,502

Ask your lender for a mortgage amortization table based on the new monthly payment. Make sure the table begins with your current balance. If you have an adjustable-rate mortgage, you'll have to ask for a new amortization schedule every time the rate changes.

One software program that compares savings based on different payment variations is sold by Banker's Secret (800-255-0899; $25 plus $3 for shipping and handling). If you wish, you can use a financial calculator to create your own schedule.

In most cases this method is the fastest, because you need to write only one check. If your lender's policy requires a second check for the prepayment amount, however, consider the second method.

▪ **Make one extra payment.** You may find it less time-consuming to prepay principal with a single lump-sum check once a year instead of writing a check a month. On a $100,000, 10.5 percent, thirty-year mortgage, $500 paid at the end of each year will knock six years off your loan and save $51,145 in interest.

No matter which method you choose, indicate on your check that your extra payment is "to be applied to principal." If your coupon has a place for prepayments, fill that in, too. A few days after your first prepayment, call and ask what your principal balance is.

Keep copies of your canceled checks until the loan is completely paid.

Note: Making optional principal payments doesn't allow you to skip your regular monthly payment.

As a rule, mortgages no longer carry a penalty for prepayment. Where there are penalties, they generally apply only during the first three to five years or if you prepay more than 20 percent of the loan balance in any twelve-month period. FHA and VA loans can be prepaid at any time without penalty. Check your mortgage agreement, or call your lender to find out if any restrictions apply.

THE TAX MYTH

Ever since Congress stripped us of almost all tax shelters, we're as reluctant to lose our mortgage interest deduction as a surprised bather is to drop his towel. Fair enough. But prepaying your mortgage isn't going to affect your tax deductions for quite a while.

Your monthly payments for the first twenty years are weighted heavily on the side of interest. When you prepay, your deductions, like your interest charges, decrease slowly. On a $75,000 mortgage (10 percent for thirty years), if you prepay $25 a month, you'll pay only $14.12 less interest the first year—an increase of $3.95 in tax if you're in the 28 percent bracket.

Anyway, using the equity you're building up in your home, you can borrow to buy rental property that will generate even better write-offs.

Besides, prepaying your mortgage in itself gives you a tax break. Your equity buildup is tax-deferred. Even when you sell, you can continue to postpone the gain by buying a more expensive home or taking advantage of the $125,000 gain exclusion available to taxpayers age fifty-five or older. (A loss on the sale of your home is not deductible.)

WHEN NOT TO PREPAY

As mouth-watering as an early payoff seems, you may not want to prepay when

- your mortgage rate is 9 percent or less—the after-tax cost of a 9 percent mortgage is only 6.48 percent if you are in the 28 percent bracket (less if you pay state tax). Prepaying in that case is like investing at 6.48 percent. You should have no trouble finding investments that earn more.

- you plan to sell within three to five years—prepayment won't make an appreciable difference because your principal balance won't have time to decrease significantly.

- you can realize better savings by refinancing at a lower rate—refinancing is a good move if you can save at least two percentage points, you can trade your adjustable-rate mortgage for the security of a fixed-rate one, or you need to take equity out of your home for remodeling, college, or a second home, for example.

- you have extremely large credit card debt that takes priority—not only does credit card interest average around 19 percent, it's not even deductible. Obviously it makes more sense to retire this debt before prepaying a deductible 10 percent mortgage.

- the house is rental property—the great thing about a rental is that your tenants are making the mortgage payments (and paying the interest) for you. Use your spare cash more profitably for other investments.

Chapter 6

Ten Safe Investments You Can Make in Twenty Minutes or Less

The problem with high-flying investments is that you don't dare leave the cockpit or glance up from the instrument panel for fear they'll crash and burn. As a busy investor, you need investments that won't suddenly take a nosedive once you've gotten them off the ground.

The following investments can be trusted to fly safely on automatic pilot. You have to pop back only once a year to review your portfolio for performance and tax consequences. If you find an investment has wandered off course, ground it and take off with another on the list.

There are trade-offs. You can't expect the highest yields from the least personal involvement. But there's no reason to settle for a passbook pittance, either. The hardworking investments suggested here give you the best of both goals. Later, if you have the leisure, you can branch out into more diverse and potentially more profitable ventures.

EE SAVINGS BONDS

Don't turn that page. This isn't your father's investment anymore. Series EE savings bonds no longer have to be purchased for patriotism instead of profit. Aimed at attracting sophisticated investors, they now offer fairly competitive, variable rates. Even so, owners of savings bonds are still thought of more as Caspar Milquetoasts than Errol Flynns. But it's precisely that simplicity and safety that make these bonds ideal investments for busy investors.

Savings bonds need less maintenance than Old Faithful. Stash them someplace fireproof, and that's it. You don't have to worry about reinvesting your earnings, because EE bonds don't pay current interest. You receive your accrued interest when you cash in the bond for its full face value.

What else makes EE savings bonds so attractive?

- You can buy in for as little as $25.
- They are issued and backed by the federal government, so there's no safer investment.
- They're fast and easy to buy.
- They offer competitive interest rates.
- You pay no commissions or fees.
- No research is needed.
- The government replaces them free if they're lost, stolen, or eaten by piranhas.
- They can't be called before maturity (so you don't have to worry about reinvesting your funds).
- They provide tax benefits.

You pay half the face value (a $1,000 bond costs $500, for instance) and redeem the bond at a higher price that includes accrued interest. You can't invest more than $15,000 ($30,000 face value) in any one year. Unlike other bonds, EE bonds are never worth less than you pay for them: their prices don't vary inversely with interest rates.

EE bonds pay a variable interest rate that's adjusted every six months—on November 1 and May 1. This means they keep pace with inflation. If you hold them five years, they pay 85 percent of the average market yield of five-year Treasury securities or 6 percent, whichever is greater. However, bonds held less than five years pay reduced interest—as little as 4.16 percent if you can't hold out for one year, then rising gradually to 6 percent.

Because the rate fluctuates, it's impossible to know when an EE bond will reach face value. At most it will take twelve years, assuming a minimum return of 6 percent. But you don't have to wait until the bond reaches face value to cash it in. You can redeem it any time after six months.

EE bonds fight taxes, too. All interest is exempt from state and local taxes. This increases your effective yield, especially if you live in a high-tax state. Federal taxes on the interest can be deferred until the bonds are cashed in or mature—up to thirty years.

Even at maturity you can keep the IRS from your door by rolling over your bonds into Series HH bonds. Denominations are $500, $1,000, $5,000, and $10,000. The accumulated interest doesn't have to be reported until the HH bonds mature in ten years or are cashed in. The HH bonds pay interest semiannually, though, and taxes are due on this amount.

Saving for the future is easy with EE bonds. Time them to mature when your child enters college, for example, or when you reach retirement age. In fact, bonds bought after 1989 pay federally tax-free interest if used for your child's college tuition. *Note:* Interest is fully nontaxable only for parents with joint adjusted gross incomes of $66,200 or less ($44,150 singles, indexed for inflation).

TWENTY-MINUTE INVESTMENT CHECKLIST

✔ Before investing, call 800-US-BONDS for the current interest rate (in Washington, D.C.: USA-8888).

✔ To buy:

- Sign up for a payroll savings plan where you work. Your employer will automatically deduct from your paycheck the amount you want to set aside to buy bonds.
- If your company doesn't have such an automatic plan, visit your bank, savings and loan, credit union, or Federal Reserve Bank.
- Avoid lines by using the mails. Obtain an order form from your bank or by writing to the Bureau of Public Debt, Parkersburg, WV 26106-1328. Fill it out and enclose a check or money order for half the face amount of the EE bonds you want. Address it to either the Federal Reserve Bank branch in your district or to the Bureau of Public Debt. Call 304-420-6110 for more information about buying by mail.

✔ To follow up:

- Your bank or savings and loan can tell you the current redemption value of your bonds. Free copies of redemption value tables for bonds with face values of $50 can be obtained from the Bureau of Public Debt, Parkersburg, WV 26106-1328.

You can also buy EE bond redemption booklets for other denominations for $1.75 from the Superintendent of Documents, U.S. Government Printing Office, Washington, D.C. 20402. The price is subject to change.

CERTIFICATES OF DEPOSIT (CDs)

If you agree to surrender your money for a specified period of time, ranging from seven days to seven years, your reward is a higher interest rate than banks offer on their savings or money market accounts. The average certificate of deposit yields one-quarter to three-quarters of a percentage point more than Treasury securities of comparable maturity (the closest alternative to CDs for safety).

However, once the bank has your money, it all but throws away the key. You usually incur a substantial penalty of from one to six months' interest if you cash in your certificate early. *Note:* Some banks have begun issuing CDs that permit partial withdrawals without penalty.

Time-short investors can combine high yield, convenience, and liquidity by buying CDs through a broker. Brokerage firms buy CDs in volume from banks and savings and loans nationwide. As a result, you may be able to pick up a certificate that pays a full percentage point more than your neighborhood bank. Brokered CDs are sold, at no fee to you, for a minimum investment of $1,000 or more.

Once you've opened a brokerage account, you also benefit from another time fighter, consolidation. You won't have to open a new bank account every time you decide to switch banks to lock in a higher yield.

Another advantage of brokered CDs: You can sell your certificate without the customary bank penalty, because brokers maintain an informal resale market. If current interest rates are lower than that of your CD, you'll profit. But if yields have risen, you can lose by selling early. In that case you may choose to pay the withdrawal penalty if it's smaller.

Whether you buy through a broker or directly from a bank, CDs issued by federally insured institutions are covered for up to $100,000. (Because brokered CDs tend to be riskier, ask for the name of the issuing bank, and avoid shaky institutions). Deposit less than the ceiling amount to allow for the compounding interest. For example, in a two-year CD earning 9 percent compounded quarterly, a deposit of $83,694 or less keeps your balance within $100,000. If you have more than $100,000 to invest, split it between CDs issued by two or more banks.

Your time is required for two decisions:

- **Do you want a fixed or variable interest rate?** If you think interest rates will rise, a variable-rate CD may be the way to go. The rate on a variable is tied to an index, such as the Treasury bill rate. A variable CD offers slightly lower rates as a trade-off for its flexibility. Shop for a CD with a guaranteed minimum rate for the entire term.
- **How long do you want to tie up your money?** If you believe interest rates are near their high or about to fall, lock in a two-year CD. If you think rates will climb even higher, buy a shorter-term certificate so your money will be free for reinvestment as interest rises.

Some banks offer rate-builder CDs with interest rates that rise a set amount every six to twelve months. At the end of each period you can take your money at no penalty or leave it in at the higher rate. You may earn a smaller overall return with such a CD, though, because the bank takes the risk of interest rates falling.

What if you haven't a clue whether rates will go up, down, or sideways? Spread your cash among several CDs with due dates six months apart. As each one matures, reinvest in a higher-yielding CD if rates have climbed or in another investment if rates have fallen.

TWENTY-MINUTE INVESTMENT CHECKLIST

✔ Check your newspaper's financial pages for the bank offering the highest rate in your area.

✔ Call several local banks and brokerage firms, and ask the following questions:

- "If I invest $1,000 in a CD today, how much will I have at the end of six months or a year?" This is the best way to compare yields, because of the innumerable ways banks and brokers quote them. Exactly how much you earn depends on the CD's effective annual yield. This reflects both the interest rate and how frequently interest is compounded. Thus, the highest rate doesn't necessarily produce the highest yield.
- What's the minimum investment?
- What's the penalty for early withdrawal?
- Are partial withdrawals allowed without penalty?
- May I add to my CD balance at some later date? This can be a boon if interest rates dip below the rate on your certificate.
- How will I be notified when my CD comes due? The bank should send you a reminder several weeks beforehand. A few banks just send out your check. Others don't notify you at all—they automatically invest your money in another CD

or, worse, a passbook savings account if they don't hear from you.

✔ Beware of these misleading quotes:

- Teaser rates—an initial yield of up to 20 percent that declines drastically within a few weeks. The combined rate is usually well below average bank rates.
- Tiered rates—high advertised yields that only apply to deposits of $25,000 or more. Small savers typically earn paltry returns.
- Hypothetical yields—compound annual yields on CDs that pay simple interest or annual yields on three- and six-month CDs (there's no guarantee you'll be able to reinvest at the same rate).
- Junk CDs—offering rates too good to be true, these subordinated debentures (also called "subordinated capital notes," "lobby notes," or "community offerings") are the bank's own debt instruments. As such, they're not federally insured or even backed by any collateral. Their seemingly high yields don't begin to compensate for the risks involved. The most publicized example of the perils of "subdebt" is the Lincoln Savings & Loan scandal.

✔ Ask your bank or broker to send you an application form and written confirmation of rates, minimum deposits, maturities, and withdrawal penalties. Have your banker or broker assign you an account number by telephone. Open your account with a check made out to your account number and endorsed "for deposit only."

MONEY MARKET MUTUAL FUNDS

If yield, liquidity, and safety rank high on your list, it's hard to top money market mutual funds. In essence, money funds are mutual funds that invest solely in short-term debt securities, such as Treasury bills, commercial paper, and certificates of deposit. Tax-free money funds buy short-term municipal bonds whose interest is exempt from federal income tax.

Unlike stock and bond mutual funds, the price of money funds doesn't fluctuate. There's no risk of loss if the stock market goes haywire.

The interest rate paid by a money fund varies daily, depending on its portfolio and the cost of money. Money funds pay higher rates than bank money market funds—as much as 1.5 percent to 2 percent more. They're particularly timely because, unlike bank rates, they move with market rates as fund managers roll over maturing assets into new issues.

The minimum initial investment is usually $1,000 to $5,000. You may add $100 or more to your account or withdraw money at any time without penalty or a charge. Dividends are automatically reinvested in more shares, relieving you of time-nibbling investment decisions and compounding your return.

Money funds are extremely liquid. Most funds offer unlimited check-writing privileges, as long as each check is for $500 or more. Your funds draw interest until your check clears. There's no minimum balance requirement once the account is open. Nor does the interest rate fall if your balance drops below a certain amount.

Although most money market funds are not insured, your risk is virtually nil. But some funds are safer than others. The most conservative are funds that hold only ninety-day Treasury bills, such as the Capital Preservation Fund. This extra safety costs you a few tenths of a percent in yield, however. *Note:* Money funds managed by brokerage firms are insured up to $500,000 by the Securities Investor Protection Corporation (SIPC).

With money funds you have the luxury of dealing by

phone or by mail. For maximum time savings, invest in a money fund that belongs to a family of funds. This lets you shift into high gear quickly and transfer your cash into stock and bond funds if market conditions change.

If you're in a high tax bracket, you may earn more, after taxes, with a tax-exempt money fund. For investors in the 28 percent bracket, a tax-exempt fund with a yield of 5 percent offers the equivalent of a taxable yield of 6.94 percent (7.25 percent in the 31 percent bracket).

If you live in a state with high income tax, such as New York or California, invest in a fund that buys only municipal bonds issued by your state. Your earnings are thus triply exempt—from federal, state, and local taxes.

TWENTY-MINUTE INVESTMENT CHECKLIST

✔ Check the business section of your local newspaper for current interest rates. Or consult a newsletter that tracks money market funds, such as William Donoghue's *Money Fund Report* and *Moneyletter*, P.O. Box 540, Holliston, MA 01746. For a list of funds and their phone numbers, write to the Investment Company Institute, 1775 K St. NW, Washington, D.C. 20006.

✔ Select at least three top-yielding money markets belonging to a family of funds, such as Dreyfus, Fidelity, Scudder, T. Rowe Price, or Vanguard. The difference in yield between comparable money funds is only about half a percentage point. So pick fund families with stock and bond products you like.

✔ Call each fund's toll-free number. If you don't know the number, call directory assistance at 1-800-555-1212. Ask the fund for a prospectus and application form.

✔ Review each prospectus for the following:

• The type of debt instruments the fund invests in.

- Average maturity of the investments in the fund's portfolio. The shorter the average maturity, the faster the fund's yield rises when interest rates move up. Funds with long average maturities have the upper hand when rates head down. For maximum safety, stick to funds whose holdings have an average maturity of fifty days or less.
- The fund's track record for the past twelve months.
- Whether the fund is waiving all or part of its management fees to boost yields. If so, how long will this largesse continue? Expect the fund's high yield to drop by as much as three-quarters of a percentage point when fees are passed on to investors. In the meantime, there's no reason not to take advantage of this marketing gimmick.
- The fund's expense ratio or yearly management charge. The average ratio is around 0.7 percent. Because costs come directly out of the fund's yield, lower expenses mean higher returns.
- Conveniences, such as minimum investment and check-writing privileges. Does the fund offer any time-saving features? Dreyfus Worldwide Dollar Fund, for example, offers an "automatic asset builder" program that lets you transfer a preset amount of money from your bank account as often as twice a month. Most banks don't charge for this type of transaction, as long as you maintain the minimum required balance.

✔ Complete the application form. Check the box permitting you to transfer money from your fund to another fund in the group simply by lifting the telephone. Also sign up for wire transfers, to wire withdrawals directly to your bank account. Mail your application with a check made out to the fund.

✔ You can also set up a money fund with your stock-broker. If you trade securities, this is a useful place to keep cash between buying and selling.

BANK MONEY MARKET ACCOUNTS

If money market mutual funds are rich, buttery desserts, bank money market accounts are low-cal substitutes. The average yield is meager compared with that of money funds (as much as 2.5 percent lower), and privileges are limited. Why, then, would you pick a bank money market account off the shelf? You may prefer the comfort of dealing with a familiar bank, or you may be uneasy about investing long distance. I know that intimidates some of my clients, even though in this electronic age, funds two thousand miles away are almost as close as next door.

With both types of money markets, interest rates are tied to the rates of short-term debt instruments. However, there are some key differences:

- If your bank money market balance falls below a preset minimum (generally from $1,000 to $2,500), the interest rate on your account drops to the passbook rate. Very few money market mutual funds require a minimum balance or, if they do, the minimum is much lower.
- Bank funds are federally insured, up to $100,000 per depositor per bank.
- Banks are like ruler-wielding schoolmarms when it comes to check-writing and automatic transfers. You're limited to three checks a month, often with a $500 minimum. You may also make three other transactions a month. Exceed these limits, and your knuckles will be rapped with a fee of from $5 to $25. Some banks may even close your account if you

persist in breaking these rules. On the other hand, money market mutual funds usually permit unlimited check writing.

TWENTY-MINUTE INVESTMENT CHECKLIST

✔ Begin with your own bank. Ask about the current interest rate, last year's average rate, minimum deposit requirements, and check-writing and transfer restrictions.

✔ Call several other local banks and compare their answers.

✔ Banks are competing aggressively for your dollars, so it pays to comparison shop. Call at least three out-of-state banks to find out if higher interest rates are available elsewhere. Banks that court out-of-state depositors often have toll-free numbers and are usually listed in surveys of interest rates in such financial magazines as *Money*. Request a written confirmation of a bank's rates and minimum deposit requirements before mailing your money.

✔ To invest by mail, ask the bank to assign you an account number by telephone. Request the mailing address of the branch where you'll be doing business. Then open the account with a check made out to your account number and endorsed "for deposit only." Make sure you also receive and complete Form W-9 to prevent unwanted income tax withholding.

✔ If your chosen bank cuts its rates, write a check and move your money to another bank.

U.S. TREASURY ISSUES

Want in on a secret? There's an investment that's a snap to acquire, pays competitive rates, provides tax benefits, needs no research, and is as secure as Fort Knox. Yet it's as overlooked as the kid in *Home Alone.* Why? Maybe it's because Uncle Sam doesn't give away free toasters.

What the government *does* do is issue three virtually risk-free securities beside EE bonds—Treasury bills, bonds, and notes. They generally yield less than certificates of deposit, but they offer other attractions. For one thing, their rates are tied to the market, not set by a committee. And all income from Treasuries is exempt from state and local taxes (but not federal tax). This feature can boost your after-tax yield on Treasuries above those of certificates of deposit or taxable money market funds if you live in a high-tax state.

But the feature that lands these investments on our list is the ease of record keeping. You don't receive your Treasuries in the form of a certificate that must be safeguarded. Instead, an account is set up for you at the Federal Reserve and credited or debited as you buy more securities or they reach maturity. You receive a statement only after each change in your holdings.

Under this system, known as Treasury Direct, interest earned and payments at maturity are wired directly to your bank or brokerage house. Alternatively, you may reinvest the proceeds from your maturing Treasuries automatically for up to two years. In effect, you enjoy the benefits of a money manager without the fee.

Treasury bills operate much like EE savings bonds. The face value of a T-bill is $10,000, but the actual price is determined by auction (most bidders are banks, money markets, and institutional investors). This means you buy a $10,000 bill at a discount. The difference between the face value at maturity and the issue price is interest and is refunded to you after the auction. The refund is deposited directly into your bank account. When the bill matures, you receive the full face value of $10,000.

T-bills mature in three, six, and twelve months. The minimum investment is $10,000, with $5,000 increments.

Although you receive your T-bill interest at the time of purchase, for tax purposes it is not included in income until the bill matures.

Treasury notes mature in two to ten years and pay a fixed rate of interest twice a year. The longer the note's maturity, the higher the interest rate. Notes that mature in two or three years sell for $5,000 or more. For notes with longer maturity dates, the minimum investment is $1,000.

Sold in $1,000 denominations, *Treasury bonds* mature in ten to thirty years. They also pay interest twice a year.

For all Treasury securities, it's wise to stagger maturity dates for steady income and quick reflexes if interest rates accelerate or brake suddenly.

Although Treasury securities are easily sold, one drawback is that you run the risk of loss if you're forced to sell notes and bonds prematurely. That's because a steep rise in interest rates can drive down the price of your securities before maturity. Don't use your emergency cash reserve to buy T-notes and T-bonds. T-bills, on the other hand, are more liquid, because their rates are short-term and fluctuate less.

If you buy a "used" T-note or T-bond on the secondary market (that is, after it has been sold through Treasury auction), you'll pay less than its par value, or a discount, if interest rates have risen since it was issued. On the other hand, if rates have fallen, you'll pay more than the original price, or a premium. This premium may be deducted on your tax return over the number of years left until maturity. Or you may elect to write off the premium as a capital loss in the year you redeem the security. Consult your tax adviser.

TWENTY-MINUTE INVESTMENT CHECKLIST

✔ Call the Bureau of Public Debt, 202-287-4088, for current interest rates, or check your local newspaper or *The Wall Street Journal* for the daily listing of prices and yields. These quotes are for large denominations but will put you in the ballpark. The "asked" price is what it costs you to buy, and the "bid" price is what you would get if you wanted to sell. For Treasury notes and bonds worth less than $25,000, ask prices will be slightly higher and bid prices lower. "Yield to maturity" is the rate of return if you hold the note or bond until it matures and reinvest all interest payments at that rate.

Treasury bills are quoted somewhat differently. The most important figure about a bill is its yield. This yield is computed on the amount you actually invest, not on the bill's face value. For example, if you send in $10,000 and are refunded $600 as up-front interest, your actual investment is $9,400 and your yield is 6.38 percent ($600/$9,400).

✔ The speediest way to buy is through your stockbroker or bank. Expect to pay $25 to $50 for the convenience, however. Most discount brokers don't handle Treasuries. Be prepared to pay for the securities when you order. Unlike a stock or bond purchase, this transaction doesn't take five days to settle.

In dealing with a bank, make sure the T-bill you're buying is a *true* Treasury bill. Some financial institutions offer "T-bill" accounts, which are actually certificates of deposit. Unless a Treasury bill is purchased from the Federal Reserve Bank, the interest you earn won't be exempt from state and local tax.

✔ Treasuries are one instance where it takes more time to deal by mail. However, if saving time means less to you than saving fees, you can buy directly from a Federal Reserve Bank or the Bureau of the Public Debt.

- Obtain a tender offer form from your local Federal Reserve Bank or from the Bureau of Public Debt, Securities Transaction Branch, Washington, D.C. 20226.
- Watch for a notice of offering in your daily newspaper. Three- and six-month T-bills are auctioned every Monday, except holidays, and one-year bills every month on the Thursday following the fourth Friday. Notes and bonds go on sale monthly and quarterly (respectively) and are announced four to six business days before the offering.
- Fill out the tender form and enclose payment for the full face amount of the security. There's no service charge. Pay with a certified personal check, cashier's check, a Treasury security redemption check, or Treasuries you own that will mature by the new issue date. Make your check payable to the Federal Reserve Bank or Branch to which you're submitting your tender. If your tender is going directly to the Treasury, your check must be made payable to the Bureau of the Public Debt.
- Where the form asks "Bid Type," check the box labeled "Noncompetitive," meaning you'll accept the average auction price.
- In the section headed "Direct Deposit Information," write your bank's nine-digit identifying number in the space labeled "Routing Number" (found at the bottom of your check or deposit slip). Then list the name of your bank, your account number, and the name on your account.
- Write on the envelope that this is a "Tender for Treasury Securities."
- Mail your tender form to the Federal Reserve Bank (or Branch) or to the Bureau of the Public Debt, Washington, D.C. 20239-1500.

✔ Your bid must be postmarked no later than the day before the auction.

✔ If there's a good chance you won't hold your securities to maturity, you're better off buying through a broker or bank. Otherwise, selling requires extra bookkeeping that costs you time and adds to your risk in a volatile bond market.

✔ For more information, send for a booklet entitled *Buying Treasury Securities at Federal Reserve Banks* (Federal Reserve Bank of Richmond, Public Services Dept., Box 27622, Richmond, VA 23261; $4.50).

GINNIE MAE CERTIFICATES

Why not enjoy the pleasure and the profit of being on the receiving instead of the paying end of mortgage payments? Check out Ginnie Maes. These pools of home mortgages, packaged and guaranteed by the Government National Mortgage Association (GNMA), offer convenience and high yields with no risk of default.

Lenders bundle up these mortgages backed by either the Veterans Administration or the Federal Housing Administration and sell them to the government. All mortgages in a pool must be on the same type of dwelling, carry the same rate of interest, and have approximately the same maturity. The GNMA reviews the loans to make sure they pass muster, then okays the package.

Brokers split up the package into certificates. Each certificate gives you a share in a specific mortgage pool, which usually totals at least $1 million. You need $25,000 to buy a single Ginnie Mae. Additional certificates may be purchased in increments of $5,000. Older Ginnie Maes go for $10,000.

If $25,000 is too rich for your budget, you may find investment satisfaction in a Ginnie Mae mutual fund or unit investment trust instead (see next two sections).

How do Ginnie Maes work? As homeowners make their monthly mortgage payments, the money is passed on to you as a certificate holder. Unlike other bonds, Ginnie Mae payments include both interest on your investment and a return of your principal. The initial monthly payments are almost entirely interest, but over time the principal component increases until the final payments are almost entirely principal. (Only the interest portion of each payment is taxed.)

Ginnie Maes enjoy the same ironclad U.S. government backing as ten-year Treasury notes but typically yield about a percentage point more. Along with this safety—unusual for an investment in mortgages—you also get liquidity. Ginnie Mae certificates trade freely in the secondary market.

The market price of a Ginnie Mae depends on its coupon, or interest rate. A low-coupon certificate sells at a discount—that is, below face value. A high-coupon certificate sells at a premium—for more than face value.

The total return on a Ginnie Mae, therefore, equals interest income plus your expected gain on a certificate selling at a discount (or minus your loss if you bought at a premium).

The sooner a low-coupon certificate is paid off, the better, because the lion's share of your return comes from the difference between the face value and the market price you paid. On the other hand, the bulk of your return on a high-coupon Ginnie Mae comes from interest payments. So a slow payoff is better.

If you think interest rates are coming down, buy a lower-coupon Ginnie Mae. Do the opposite if you think rates are going up. Why? If rates are falling, the low-coupon Ginnie Mae will be repaid faster, increasing its yield to maturity. If rates are rising, the high-coupon certificate will be paid back more slowly, again increasing its yield to maturity.

HANDLE WITH CARE

For all their fine qualities, Ginnie Maes are tricky and often misunderstood. Yes, they *are* government-guaranteed, but only against late mortgage payments and foreclosures. You aren't shielded against these hazards:

- **There's never a certain yield or fixed maturity.**
- **The value of Ginnie Mae certificates rises and falls daily just like other bond prices.** So if you need cash and have to sell your certificate, it might be worth more, or less, than you paid for it.
- **Return of principal prior to maturity is erratic.** Although it's better than not getting your money back, the continual return of principal exposes you to reinvestment risk.

For example, when mortgage rates drop nationwide, many homeowners rush out to refinance at lower rates. That puts more money in the pool and increases your monthly checks by substantial amounts of principal. Why is that bad? Because you probably won't be able to reinvest at the high rate paid by the original certificate.

Ginnie Maes can also be paid off early when a home changes hands, and lower mortgage rates stimulate real estate sales.

Prepayment reduces the life of the mortgage pool. The average life of a pool based on thirty-year mortgages is only twelve years, while certificates backed by fifteen-year loans have an average life of just seven years. As a result, your total income may be far less than you anticipated.

Investment caution is therefore advised during periods of high interest rates, because chances are good that a lot of mortgages will be refinanced within a few years.

■ **Ginnie Maes are "self-liquidating" investments.** When a Ginnie Mae expires, that's it. There's no final payment, because your entire principal has already been returned to you. Each month's check includes part of your original investment. If you spend the entire amount each month as if it were all interest, and don't reinvest the principal, your savings will evaporate. And reinvestment is a problem, because principal is returned in dribs and drabs or in unexpected chunks.

■ **Ginnie Mae certificates are not identical.** Because each pool of mortgages differs by region, age of loans, and the type of home financed, differences in risk can be considerable.

GINNIE MAE MUTUAL FUNDS

More than thirty mutual funds invest the bulk of their assets in Ginnie Maes, and dozens more include them among their holdings.

The main advantage of investing in Ginnie Maes through mutual funds is cost. You can buy into one of these funds for as little as $1,000 (less for Individual Retirement Accounts).

You also save on transaction costs. You'll pay from $250 to $400 to a broker to buy a $25,000 Ginnie Mae certificate, if not in commission, then in lower yield. A no-load fund costs nothing.

As with other types of mutual funds, you benefit from professional managers who know premiums from discounts and par from face value. Different Ginnie Maes are bought and sold to maximize the return on the fund. This can translate into better returns than your know-how might yield.

Fund managers pick up better bargains, too. Ginnie

Mae prices are negotiable, and broker markups are hard to detect. Spreads of Ginnie Maes traded retail often run around two points, or $20 for each $1,000 of certificate value. By purchasing large blocks of Ginnie Maes, funds get better prices.

Funds give you the option of automatically reinvesting the irregular monthly principal payments. This saves time and eliminates the danger that you'll inadvertently spend your nest egg. It also lets you accumulate shares through dollar-cost averaging.

Other advantages of mutual funds include high liquidity, the ability to switch into other types of mutual funds if returns on Ginnie Maes fall, and even free check writing.

Funds pay out of earnings—that is, interest received plus any capital gains from payoffs of the underlying mortgages. The principal is kept in your account and used to buy more Ginnie Maes.

GINNIE MAE UNIT INVESTMENT TRUSTS

A Ginnie Mae unit investment trust buys dozens of Ginnie Mae certificates. These are pools of home mortgages packaged by the Government National Mortgage Association. Brokers split the pools into certificates and sell them as securities to the public. Interest and principal payments are guaranteed by the government.

Unlike mutual funds, unit trust portfolios are fixed. The trust sponsors purchase Ginnie Maes only once, locking in a fixed return if you hold to maturity. The Ginnie Maes are held in trust by banks.

One advantage of unit trusts is lower management fees, because trust portfolios aren't actively managed.

On the down side, these units rise and fall in value with interest rates, just as single certificates do. If you want to sell a unit purchased before a rise in interest rates, you'll find the unit worth less than when you bought it.

Another negative is that monthly dividend and principal payments can't be reinvested directly, because the trust's portfolio is closed. And no-load trusts are unavailable. Almost all unit trusts levy an up-front sales charge of 3 percent to 5 percent.

TWENTY-MINUTE INVESTMENT CHECKLIST

CERTIFICATES

✔ For a free pamphlet on investing in Ginnie Maes, write to GNMA, Suite 1600, 451 Seventh St. SW, Washington, D.C. 20410.

✔ Check current rates in the financial pages of your newspaper and compare them with those of U.S. Treasury securities. The rates are shown as coupons. In the next two columns, to the right of the coupons, are the bid and ask prices of the certificates. In the fourth column you'll find the annual yield (based on a twelve-year life span).

✔ Call at least three stockbrokers:

- Tell them the coupon rate and other characteristics you want.
- Ask for quotes on pools that interest you.
- Compare the actual cost with the amount quoted in the newspaper.
- Ask for an explanation of how the yield is computed.
- Find out whether the broker charges a commission or marks up the price.

✔ Purchase the certificate through the broker offering the best buy. Try to get a certificate in a pool of $100 million or more for less volatility.

MUTUAL FUNDS

✔ Call at least three funds (use their toll-free numbers), and ask for a prospectus and application form. Some suggestions:

- Premier GNMA (800-242-8671)
- Oppenheimer GNMA (800-525-7048)
- Dreyfus GNMA (800-782-6620)
- Smith Barney U.S. Government (800-544-7835)
- Vanguard Fixed-Income GNMA (800-662-7447)

✔ Check the prospectus for the following:

- Is at least 65 percent of the fund's portfolio invested in Ginnie Maes? Don't consider any fund that doesn't meet this test.
- How are the rest of the fund's assets invested? For example, does it invest in Treasuries (safe) or directly in mortgages (risky)? Are you comfortable with the fund's level of risk?
- Is it a no-load or load fund?
- What's the minimum investment required?
- Are there transaction fees?
- In the table showing historic per-share results, look for the line item listing dividends from interest or investment income. This amount was paid out to investors. The increase or decrease in net asset value (NAV) shows how much the share prices fluctuated in addition to dividend payouts.
- What was the fund's total return over the past five years, ten years?

✔ Fill out the application blank, and mail with a check for the amount you want to invest.

UNIT INVESTMENT TRUSTS

✔ Call at least three brokerage firms and ask for a trust prospectus and an application form.

✔ Compare trust yields, management fees, transaction fees, and amount of up-front sales load.

✔ Check prospectus for the minimum investment.

✔ Fill out the application blank and mail with a check for the amount you want to invest.

STOCK MUTUAL FUNDS

If you want a stake in American business, but you're too busy to research and choose your own stocks, invest in a mutual fund. A mutual fund is a company that pools money from thousands of investors to buy and sell securities. You buy shares in the fund, making you a part owner of its portfolio and entitling you to a portion of its earnings.

In the game of one-upmanship, mutual funds are clear winners over individual stocks. With mutual funds you need only a few thousand dollars to put together the kind of sophisticated portfolio once available only to the wealthy.

Other major advantages are

- Full-time professional management—the fund's stocks are monitored, and buy-sell decisions are made daily, sparing you the work.
- Diversification—your money is spread among the hundreds of securities the fund owns, so a plunge in the price of one holding creates scarcely a ripple in the value of your investment. For further protection, diversify by building a portfolio of funds that survive, and thrive, under a variety of market conditions, such as a blue-chip stock fund, a small company fund, and an international portfolio.

  Although diversification is a cushion, it's no guarantee against a fall. The price of mutual fund shares fluctuates just as those of stocks do. In the October

1987 crash, the average stock mutual fund plummeted 20.9 percent, almost as much as the market as a whole.

- Minimal paperwork—you receive reports and earnings from only one company.
- Liquidity—selling your mutual fund shares is generally quick and easy.
- Variety—whether you seek income or growth, prefer health care over technology, or favor the Southwest over the Northeast, there's a fund for you, roughly 2,100 in all.

You can buy into most funds for as little as $1,000. Some have no minimum at all. Once you're a shareholder, you can usually add more shares for a minimum $100 investment, because funds offer fractional shares. (To invest round amounts regularly in individual stocks is almost impossible.) If you wish, you can sign up for automatic reinvestment of your dividends. Count on putting in two hours a month managing each fund.

Plan to hold your mutual fund shares for at least five years, to give your fund time to rebound from any downturns. If you think you might need the money sooner, stick to low-risk funds.

For convenience and one-stop shopping, invest in a family of funds—an investment company that operates several stock, bond, and money market funds as a group. Among the better-known fund families are Dreyfus, Fidelity, Putnam, T. Rowe Price, and Vanguard. Most fund families provide such shareholder services as

- **Telephone switching.** You can quickly move cash from one fund to another within the family if the market dives or you change your strategy from income to growth. Some funds limit you to three or four switches a year, which should be plenty. Otherwise you'll spend too much time monitoring your selections. Bear in mind that each switch is a taxable transaction, unless your cash is in an IRA.

- **Automatic purchase plans.** The fund company debits your savings or checking account regularly and invests that money in your chosen portfolio. This lets you take advantage of dollar-cost averaging (see chapter 5, page 86).
- **Dividend reinvestment plans.** The compounding effect of automatically plowing dividends back into savings can be dramatic. Dividends can be reinvested in another of the family's funds—for example, income from your stock fund can be deposited in your money market account.
- **Check-writing privileges.** This can be a boon or a bugbear, depending on your willpower. Remember, too, that on a stock mutual fund, every check you write must be reported on your tax return as a capital gain or loss.
- **Shareholder statements.** Mutual funds relieve you of record keeping. Every time you reap a dividend or buy or sell shares, you receive a statement showing the activity in your account. Some funds even compute your capital gains or losses on fund investments at tax time. *Note:* For tax purposes, keep year-end cumulative statements for as long as you hold shares in that fund.

No-load mutual funds are bought directly from the fund sponsor by phone or by mail. For this reason you pay no sales charges. Load funds are sold by stockbrokers and financial planners, who collect a sales charge of up to 8.5 percent of your initial investment. That means if you invest $10,000, only $9,150 would find its way into the fund. The other $850 would line your broker's pocket.

Studies have shown that no-load and load funds perform equally well. Invest in a load fund, therefore, only if you want the personal services of a professional or you decide a particular load fund best meets your investment goals.

TWENTY-MINUTE INVESTMENT CHECKLIST

✔ Write for the *Guide to Mutual Funds*, a list of stock funds and their phone numbers published by the Investment Company Institute, 1600 M St. NW, Suite 600, Washington, D.C. 20036. The cost is $5. Also watch for the periodic rankings of funds published in *Barron's, Money,* or *Forbes.*

✔ Select at least five funds that match the goals you set in chapter 4, and call each fund's toll-free number for a current prospectus and an annual or quarterly report. Study the following:

- The fund's objectives. The Investment Company Institute lists twenty-two fund goals (for example, growth and income, maximum capital gains, and balanced).
- How the fund plans to achieve its goal. The management policies section of the prospectus reflects the fund's personality—its intended investments (stocks, precious metals, global securities), how much it may invest in any one industry, and its guidelines regarding the quality of investments.
- The risk section. What types of risk will management take? For example, does it rule out the use of options or leverage? Does it stake its fortune on new ventures or venerable institutions? Can you tolerate the level of risk?

- The background of the officers and directors. By-pass funds with recent changes in management or whose officers clearly lack experience.
- The fund's operating expenses. Does the fund levy a load or charge you to buy, reinvest, or redeem shares? What are the annual operating expenses? The average stock fund has an expense ratio of 1.3 percent (that is, for each $10,000 in assets, the fund pays out $130 in annual overhead costs). The expense ratio appears in the "Fee Table" or "Summary of Expenses" section of the prospectus. Avoid funds whose administrative, advisory, or marketing expenses, called "12b-1" fees, exceed 1.5 percent of their assets. (Newspaper tables of mutual fund prices carry notations showing which funds charge 12b-1 fees.)
- How to buy and redeem shares. What's the minimum required purchase and redemption amount? Some funds levy back-end loads or exit fees when you redeem your shares. Back-end loads generally begin at about 5 percent and decline gradually over seven years; exit fees remain at a fixed 1 percent or 2 percent. What is the procedure for cashing in?
- The performance table. Zero in on the fund's total return, not its current yield. Total return takes into account fluctuations in the fund's share price, as well as income. If a fund yielded an impressive 15 percent, but its price dropped 12 percent, its total return to investors is a pitiful 3 percent.

This performance table also shows per-share dividends, capital gains distributions, and share price at the beginning and end of the year. Check the portfolio turnover rate. Generally, the higher the rate, the greater the fund's expenses. A rate that tops 60 percent is high.

Remember that past performance is no guarantee of return in the future. Look for consistent long-term performance rather than spectacular short-term highs.

- A fund's five- and ten-year track records compared with other funds sharing the same objective.
- Warnings. If the prospectus even hints of possible trouble, such as lawsuits or SEC investigations, burn it.

✔ For a listing of the securities each fund owns, ask for the fund's Statement of Additional Information.

✔ If it's a load fund, call your broker. If it's a no-load fund, complete the application form and mail with a check for your initial investment. Some funds take your information over the phone and send you the application to sign. Brokers also do the paperwork for you. If the fund is part of a family of funds, apply for telephone exchange and other privileges at the same time.

Tip: Switch a small amount of money from one fund to another after your account has been set up to make sure everything works smoothly.

✔ Save time as a shareholder by calling your fund at off-peak hours. Most funds are busiest in the middle of the day, especially on Mondays. Some fund families, such as Fidelity, provide round-the-clock phone service for customers.

Jot down the details of telephone exchanges—the time, date, name of the person who took your order, account number, and dollar amount. If the fund assigns a transaction number to the order, make a note of it.

Tear out the page of the prospectus explaining redemptions and keep it for reference. Some suggestions to speed the process of bailing out:

- Choose a fund with a money market fund in its family. Then arrange to exchange from one to the other when you first join the fund. This gives you access to your money within three days after the exchange, using the money market's checks.

- Sign up for telephone redemption, if available.
- Ask the fund to wire redemptions to your bank. Your redemption letter should include the bank's name, address, and routing number (shown on the bottom of your checks), your account number, and whether the account is checking or savings. Prepare the letter ahead of time, leaving the date blank.

   Tip: To minimize taxable gains and maximize losses, redeem your highest-priced shares first. Specify the block of shares you want to sell in your redemption letter to the fund.

- If your fund requires a signature guarantee from your bank or broker, obtain it in advance.
- Send your redemption letter by Express Mail or other overnight courier.
- Open an account with Charles Schwab, the discount broker, and use its Mutual Fund Marketplace to trade shares.

Mutual funds must send you the sale proceeds within seven calendar days of their receipt of the proper forms.

BLUE-CHIP STOCKS

Blue chips are the aristocracy of stocks. Like old money, they have staid and venerable reputations to maintain. They can be trusted with the long-term care of your capital. A brief glance at stock prices every few months is all that's necessary.

Blue-chip companies have long, proven earnings records, an unbroken history of paying quarterly cash dividends for twenty-five years or more, well-known products with leading market shares, stable manage-ment, and low debt. These big-name companies include AT&T, Coca-Cola, Dow Chemical, DuPont, General Electric, General Motors, Kodak, Procter & Gamble, Quaker Oats, 3M, Sears, and Westinghouse.

Besides paying dividends, blue chips have excellent capital gains potential. These aren't hotshot growth stocks, however, so don't expect overnight profits. These low-risk stocks generally take time to appreciate.

If you have enough cash, diversify your holdings among leaders in different industries.

TWENTY-MINUTE INVESTMENT CHECKLIST

✔ Study the company's annual report, its *Value Line* or *Standard & Poor's* listing at your library, and the fifty-two-week high and low shown in your newspaper's financial pages. Try to buy at a historical low or middle point.

✔ Buy shares through your stockbroker. If you know which blue chips you want to buy, use a discount bro-ker and save 50 percent to 75 percent on commissions.

✔ Sign up for a dividend reinvestment plan if of-fered, and automatically buy extra shares without extra commissions (see chapter 5).

ZERO-COUPON BONDS

Ideal for the time-pressed investor, zero-coupon bonds let you lay out a relatively modest sum today and re-ceive an impressive amount at a specified date in the future. Nothing beats them for predictability. You know in advance exactly how much you'll come into when the bond reaches maturity. And best of all, zero-coupon bonds require no management. You make a onetime purchase and lock them away in a safe place for ten to twenty years. They pay no current interest, so you don't have to reinvest.

When you buy a zero, you own a bond's interest coupon, just as if it were a share of stock. All of the bond's interest will be paid out in a lump sum at maturity. That means there are no semiannual interest payments, as there are with other bonds. The bond's maturity could be from six months to thirty years away. The more distant the bond's maturity date, the lower your purchase price.

You buy the bond at a substantial discount from its $1,000 face value. For example, a zero-coupon bond yielding 8.5 percent that matures in twenty years might cost $189, compared with its $1,000 face value. The $811 difference between your cost and the face value is, in effect, accumulated interest. You get this interest only when you cash in the bond.

You must pay tax on the interest as it accrues, even though you won't see the money for years. For this reason zeros are a good choice for tax-deferred investments, such as a Keogh, IRA, or your child's Uniform Gifts to Minors custodian account. You can also avoid this "phantom interest" by buying zero-coupon municipal bonds, issued by states and municipalities. These are exempt from federal tax and, if you're a resident of the issuing state, from state and local tax as well.

Make sure you won't need the money before the bond's maturity. The prices of long-term zeros are about three times as volatile as those of ordinary bonds. A one-point rise in interest rates can create a double-digit loss if you're forced to sell early.

For this reason the best use of zeros is to provide cash for a future need, such as sending your child to college or your silver-lined retirement. Thus, for example, if you estimate you'll need $28,000 for your child's tuition in ten years, you can invest $12,000 or so in ten-year zero-coupon bonds yielding 8.25 percent and be certain of receiving the bonds' face value of $28,000 in time for freshman registration.

If you aren't investing for a special purpose, reduce the likelihood of having to sell the bond prematurely by sticking with maturities of seven years or less.

Be wary of callable bonds, which can be redeemed by the issuer before they mature. Once you've locked in a good interest rate for the right length of time, you want to hold the bond to maturity. You don't want to waste time searching for a new investment, especially one that may not have as high a yield. Check the prospectus to see if the bond is callable according to an "accretion schedule." *Note:* Zeros issued by the Treasury Department can't be called prior to maturity.

Safety should be a prime concern. You're banking on the distant future. You can't collect the $1,000 if the issuer has long since gone bankrupt. Your best bet are zero-coupon Treasury bonds (sometimes known as TIGRs, CATS, and STRIPS) or federally insured zero certificates of deposit.

STRIPS are the safest of all zeros and the easiest to sell in a hurry. An acronym for separate trading of registered interest and principal of securities, STRIPS are Treasury bonds the government itself has stripped of their coupons. Because they're a direct obligation of the U.S. government, STRIPS yield up to a tenth of a percentage point less than TIGRs or CATS.

TIGRs and CATS are Treasury bonds that brokers have purchased, stripped, and then resold to investors. TIGR is an acronym for Merrill Lynch's Treasury investment growth receipts. CATS (certificates of accrual on Treasury securities) are Salomon Brothers' version of TIGRs. These securities behave like zero-coupon bonds but are actually certificates issued by custodian banks—

Manufacturers Hanover in the case of TIGRs and Morgan Guaranty for CATS—which hold the bonds in trust.

Less than 100 percent safe are zeros issued by corporations and municipalities and those backed by mortgages. Avoid zero-coupon unit trusts or bond funds because they charge high sales fees and often invest in riskier zero-coupon corporate junk bonds.

TWENTY-MINUTE INVESTMENT CHECKLIST

✔ Most zeros trade on the over-the-counter market. Check the financial section of your local newspaper or *The Wall Street Journal* for current price quotes. If you're interested in TIGRs, call your local Merrill Lynch broker.

✔ All zeros, including Treasury zeros, are marketed by brokers. TIGRs can be purchased only from Merrill Lynch. Call at least three full-service or discount brokers and ask the following:

- How much must I invest for the zero I want?
- How much will my investment be worth at maturity?
- What is the effective yield to maturity? Ask each broker if he adds an extra commission after he's calculated the yield. If so, have him recompute the yield, taking the extra commission into account.

The broker with the lowest figure for the first question and the highest for the other two is offering the best deal.

✔ Find out if there's an active secondary market for your particular zero.

✔ Ask whether a municipal or corporate bond is callable. If a zero can be called, ask for both its yield to maturity and its yield to call (your guaranteed return if the bond must be redeemed early). It's best, however, to buy only noncallable zeros, for their guaranteed yield.

✔ If you're considering corporate or municipal zeros, review the issuer's financial stability. Buy only zeros that are triple-A rated by *Moody's* or *Standard & Poor's*. Some municipals come with insurance, which lowers your yield by about half a percentage point.

✔ If you're considering a zero certificate of deposit, make sure the certificate is federally insured.

✔ Before investing, ask the broker to compare the zero's yield with the current return on straight Treasury bonds. If the zero is not offering a higher yield, don't buy at this time.

SINGLE-PREMIUM LIFE AND UNIVERSAL LIFE II INSURANCE

These modern types of life insurance provide an effortless way for the busy, high-tax-bracket investor to build up tax-deferred earnings. Because they're primarily investment vehicles, the insurance coverage is minimal. Don't buy either of these types of policies to meet your life insurance needs.

With single-premium life, you make a lump-sum premium payment, which ranges from $5,000 to $500,000. Most of your premium is invested, while a small portion goes toward insurance coverage. The income the policy earns is tax-deferred.

Universal life II offers both payment and investment flexibility. You can change both the premium payments and the amount of the death benefit, within limits, from year to year. This lets you cut back on premiums in years when you're short on cash and double down on your investing when interest rates are high. This type of policy usually provides more insurance coverage and lower savings (cash value) than single-premium life.

With single-premium whole life, the insurance company makes all the investment decisions for you. You're guaranteed a minimum rate of return on the cash value, usually around 4 percent.

With single-premium variable life and universal life II, the company lets you decide where to invest your principal—in stocks, bonds, or money market mutual funds. For this reason there's no guaranteed rate of return. These policies offer all the conveniences of a large mutual fund family. You can assume as much or as little risk as you want, diversify among different kinds of funds, and be conservative or aggressive by turns as market conditions change.

Single-premium life is an excellent way to borrow. You may generally borrow up to 75 percent of the cash value during the first year and up to 90 percent thereafter. Although the insurer charges an interest rate of around 8 percent, the actual cost of the loan is zero. That's because the interest is considered equal to your return on the amount borrowed.

You don't get off tax free, however. The amount of cash you borrow or withdraw from your single-premium policy is taxed to the extent of policy earnings. You're also subject to a 10 percent penalty on loans or withdrawals before age 59½, unless you become disabled. *Note:* A new single-premium product called "seven-pay life" sidesteps the rule against tax-free borrowing.

(Be warned that policy loans come out of your survivors' pockets if you die with a balance due.)

Caution: Be sure you understand the sales charges. These run as high as 9 percent and can drastically reduce or even eliminate your return if you cash in the policy early. So don't commit cash you'll need any time soon. It takes at least ten years for your investment income to exceed the commissions and fees deducted by the insurer.

Beware, too, of high surrender charges if you take out your money during the first seven to ten years. If you let the policy lapse, all interest it's earned becomes immediately taxable.

Tax benefits are the major appeal of these types of insurance. Returns tend to be lower than with other investments. In fact, if you don't need insurance and want liquidity, a municipal bond mutual fund may be a more attractive investment.

TWENTY-MINUTE INVESTMENT CHECKLIST

✔ Check the ratings of insurers in A. M. Best's guide, *Best's Insurance Reports, Life-Health Edition.* Your public library should have a copy. Invest only with a company that has at least $1 billion in assets and an A or A+ rating from A. M. Best. About 190 insurers have earned an A+ rating for ten years straight. For a list of these top performers, send $10 to Insurance Forum, P.O. Box 245, Ellettsville, IN 47429.

✔ Call five insurance companies that meet the above standard, and read their literature carefully. Zero in on the following:

- Premium payments. For universal life II, how are they calculated and what is the highest payment you may have to make to maintain your policy?
- How much of your premium goes to cash value?
- Cash surrender values. How much can you expect to collect after one year, three years, five years, and so on?

- The *net* interest rate—that is, the return after deducting both the cost of insurance coverage and administrative expenses.
- Is the high advertised rate a come-on? How long is a fixed policy's initial interest rate guaranteed? May you bail out with no penalty if rates fall by a preset amount, usually one percentage point?
- The guaranteed minimum rate of return.
- The guaranteed death benefit if the portfolio you've invested your premiums in shows a loss.
- Administrative expenses. What are the front-end commissions, portfolio management charges, mortality expenses (which rise as you age), and surrender charges? These fees can erode your return by as much as 2.5 percent each year. Avoid any policy whose surrender charges don't phase out within seven years.
- What interest rate is charged on policy loans? Generally, a net interest of 2 percent to 4 percent is charged on your original investment; earnings may be borrowed free of charge.
- Cost-index numbers—the smaller the index number, the lower the cost.
- For single-premium variable and universal II life policies, the variety of investment choices and switching privileges. Deal only with companies that let you choose from at least five different investment funds.
- For single-premium whole-life policies, the insurer's investment fund's track record over the last three years.

✔ Discuss any questions with your insurance agent, stockbroker, or financial planner. Listen to any sales pitch skeptically: ask about interest rates, mortality

rates, and refunds of charges. Are projections realistic—
for example, is it likely the interest rate will remain at 10
percent for twenty years or that policyholders will increasingly live longer despite new diseases such as
AIDS?

✔ Buy your policy from one of the three professionals mentioned previously or from the insurance company directly.

✔ If you have second thoughts after applying, you
have ten days after you receive your policy to return it
for a full refund.

Chapter 7

How to Build Wealth Without Spending a Second or a Cent

My sister called me the other night. She's a zealously professional engineer with an aerospace firm that had just finished putting together a contract proposal for a large project.

"I missed the whole summer," she moaned. "Here I am, living at the beach, and I've spent every day of the last two months in a building with no windows."

I knew that when she was working on a proposal, she rarely got home before ten, even on weekends. She didn't even see daylight at mealtimes—food was catered in.

We chatted awhile, catching up, and then she said, "I've been going over my bank statements, and this is interesting—while I was working on the proposal, my ATM withdrawals averaged two hundred dollars a month. But now that it's ended, I'm taking out two hundred a *week*."

Obviously the crucial element was time. Give her the time and she spent the money. Simply by being busy, she had been saving $600 a month.

So instead of worrying that you're too busy to manage your money, be grateful you're too busy to spend it. It turns out you can travel the road to riches without lifting a finger. In fact, doing nothing is the only requirement:

- Don't open a mail-order catalog.
- Don't tune in to the Home Shopping Network.
- Don't follow garage sale arrows.
- Don't go near a galleria, factory outlet, or minimall.

For every eighteen-karat gold chain, sleeping cat doorstop, and bargain-basement sale you miss, you'll put $25 to $100 in your pocket. Before long, doing nothing will do plenty to help you achieve financial success.

Not only that, you'll save lots of time as well—time spent crawling in traffic, time spent circling for parking, time spent scanning the tabloids at checkout counters.

A DOLLAR SAVED

These days a penny saved is a waste of time, but a dollar saved—well, thanks to the Sixteenth Amendment, establishing the income tax, a dollar saved is $1.50 earned.

It's all because of your tax bracket. In theory the federal tax law has only three rates—15 percent, 28 percent, and a top rate of 31 percent. But with exemption and itemized deduction phaseouts, your federal tax bracket can rise as high as *35 percent*. The tax you pay is an average of these rates. If you earn $40,000 and pay $8,000 in income tax, for example, you're paying an average of 20 percent. This doesn't mean you're in the 20 percent bracket. Your tax bracket is the rate on which the last dollars you earn are taxed. That's the rate you need to consider in making financial decisions.

Of course, federal income tax is merely the most notorious of our levies. On top of that, 7.65 percent is abducted for Social Security tax (15.3 percent if you are self-employed). Then a healthy percentage is siphoned off for state and city income taxes, not to mention sales and property taxes. In football, they call it "piling on."

Only federal, state, and local income taxes count in figuring your tax bracket, however. For the purposes of this section, let's assume you're in the 40 percent bracket. That means

- if you're granted a $1,200 raise, you'll take home $720.
- a Treasury bill paying 7 percent interest nets only 4.2 percent.
- a tax-exempt bond paying 6 percent is equivalent to a taxable bond yielding 10 percent.
- you must earn $1.67 to recoup every $1.00 you spend. For example, if you plan to buy $100 tickets to *Phantom of the Opera* next month, but decide to rent the Lon Chaney video version for $3 instead, you'll save $97. To *earn* $97 for your savings account, you'd have to make $162.

Moral: The most efficient—and time-saving—way to accumulate investment funds is to *spend less* rather than to earn more.

THE TIME VALUE OF SAVINGS

As you race around trying to beat the clock, time seems like your worst enemy. Ironically, in the savings game, time is your best ally.

Time can perform a special-effects job on your savings that Industrial Light and Magic would envy. Deposit

$5,000 in a savings account paying a mere 6 percent and wait forty years. When you finally creak open the vault, $51,429 will spill out. Let's see Steven Spielberg top that.

Time's secret weapon is compound interest. Consider Benjamin Wick of Seattle. At the age of three months he joined the work force when his photograph was published in a mail-order catalog. His savvy grandparents immediately invested his $2,000 earnings in his own tax-deferred IRA account. If the account earns 12 percent, Benjamin's IRA will be worth a staggering $1.6 million when he retires to Scottsdale at age 59½.

Even if you don't get a two-decade jump on retirement, time will produce impressive results. Let's say you contribute $2,000 a year to a retirement plan, and it grows tax free at the rate of 12 percent annually. In ten years your $20,000 investment will grow to $28,886. After fifteen years, having contributed $30,000, you'll have $63,613 (quite a jump in five years), and in twenty years your $40,000 will more than triple to $124,813.

Retirement plans produce such dramatic results because their earnings grow tax free. But even taxes can't put a damper on time. The same $2,000 invested every year in a taxable mutual fund earning 12 percent will put a nearly as impressive $90,174 in your pocket in twenty years.

TIMING IS EVERYTHING

Nothing illustrates the time value of money better than the difference between contributing to your IRA on January 1 of the tax year or April 15 of the following year. If you wait until April 15, you're passing up 15½ months of compounding. And compounding is the magic act of finance.

The following table shows the power of time:

Accumulation after Thirty Years
(9% annual return)

Annual contribution	Investment on January 1	Investment the following April 15	Difference
$2,000 Individual	$297,150	$264,098	$33,052
$2,250 Married Couple	$334,294	$297,110	$37,184
$4,000 Working Couple	$594,301	$528,196	$66,105

Startling, isn't it? Merely contributing the same amount in the same investment 15½ months apart makes a difference of over $1,000 a year. If that doesn't give you a sense of urgency, nothing will. Even if you can't make the full contribution on January 1, invest as much as you can as early as possible.

ONE LUMP OR TWENTY?

If time works wonders with gradual investment, think what it can do with a lump sum. We've seen above how investing $2,000 a year at 12 percent nets you $28,886 in ten years. But what if you invest a single lump sum of $20,000, then sit back and wait ten years? The result would be $62,117—a stunning difference.

The more you set aside now, the greater your gain, even at the same interest rate. So when you think about sinking $2,000 into a big-screen TV or blowing it on penny stocks, remember: you're not just losing $2,000, you're losing its value over time.

THAT OLD NEMESIS—INFLATION

In the eternal battle of good versus evil, time is pitted against inflation. It does no good to retire with a million dollars if a loaf of bread costs three thousand dollars. In determining how much you need to invest to meet your goals, therefore, remember to factor in the villainous effect of inflation. Most financial planners use a 6 percent rate of inflation as a guideline. To roughly analyze an investment, deduct 6 percent from your expected rate of return before computing the time value of your money. Then throw in an adjustment for taxes, too.

It's a simple calculation. Suppose you're thinking of investing in a high-grade corporate bond yielding 11 percent. The bond matures in five years and pays annual interest. With 6 percent inflation, you will earn 5 percent (11 percent − 6 percent). If you're in the 28 percent tax bracket, you'll dutifully turn over 3.08 percent (11 percent × 28 percent) of your earnings to the IRS. The result: Your 11 percent bond actually nets 2.08 percent after inflation and taxes.

Note: Your interest possesses the superior wizardry of compounding. Inflation doesn't compound. Therefore your actual return will be rosier than the picture painted by the above calculation.

THE RULE OF 72

A tip in case you're ever caught without your calculator: To find out how long it takes to double your money, divide the rate of return into 72.

The rule of 72 assumes that interest is compounded annually. Your investment will double in still less time if interest compounds more often. Daily compounding is as powerful as dynamite. Because taxes are not taken into account, this method is more accurate for such tax-advantaged investments as IRAs and Keoghs.

Interest Rate	Years to Double
6%	72/6 = 12.0
7%	72/7 = 10.3
8%	72/8 = 9.0
9%	72/9 = 8.0
10%	72/10 = 7.2
15%	72/15 = 4.8
20%	72/20 = 3.6

SMART SAVING STRATEGIES

Saving can be as maddening as building a sand castle at high tide. The swirls and eddies of daily life steadily undermine the walls, and crisis and calamity crash like tidal waves over your defenses. It may be years before your financial fortress will protect you from hostile economic forces.

You can't chuck bucket and pail and let the surf wash away your efforts, however. Saving takes the same rigid, resigned, and dreary discipline as dieting. Whether you're counting calories or pennies, persistence pays.

There may be only one key to savings success—dogged single-mindedness—but there are several ways to speed the process and stay motivated. Nothing encourages saving more than watching your assets multiply.

The following smart saving strategies turn penny pinching into big payoffs:

■ **Save automatically.** Put a middleman between yourself and your earnings. Set up an automatic savings program to divert money out of your hands before you can spend it. These plans, include

- tax-deferred retirement plans [401(k)s]
- U.S. savings bond payroll deduction plans
- credit union payroll plans
- automatic transfers from a checking account to a savings account
- automatic transfers from a bank account to a mutual fund

■ **Squirrel away at least 10 percent of your gross pay.** Forget budgeting. Tediously tracking every dollar you spend for months on end is too time-consuming. Instead, sit down and write a check to yourself for 10 percent of your wages each and every payday. Deposit the money in a money market or stock mutual fund (you may need to add something extra to the first deposit to meet the fund's minimum requirement). Pay yourself no matter how many other creditors get short shrift.

Try to increase the percentage you save by one point each year. As retirement nears, you should be stashing away at least 20 percent of your income.

Your first savings goal should be an emergency cash reserve equal to three months' living expenses (six months if you're self-employed), in case of illness, layoff, or other financial setback.

■ **Decrease spending.** Along with the immoral and fattening, most people have a taste for the expensive. Luckily, the busier you are, the less chance you have to indulge in this vice. Still, everyone can find expenses to trim. Cutbacks in entertainment, clothing, and restaurant meals are usually the easiest.

■ **Spend wisely.** Make your money count by concentrating on purchases that genuinely improve your quality of life. Reduce spending on items that

- are perishable—vacations and disposable cameras.
- depreciate rapidly—luxury cars.
- are fads or are quickly outdated—trendy clothing and electronic equipment.
- you can live without—yogurt and pasta makers, pedicures, and diamond-studded dog collars.

Save time, gas, and money by shopping infrequently. Jot down items you need, and make just one buying trip a week or, if you can hold out, once a month. Shop for bargains, but only on items you need—don't go broke saving money.

■ **Retire costly debt.** Do so even if you have to use your savings. That sounds self-defeating, but if your money is earning 4 percent after taxes in a passbook savings account and you're paying 19 percent to buy on time, you have a negative cash flow that will soon consume all your savings and then bleed your future earnings dry, too.

To add to the hemorrhaging, the cost of consumer interest is no longer tax-deductible. For example, suppose you have $2,000 in a money market fund paying 8 percent annually. That's $160.08 a year, or $115.26 after taxes if you're in the 28 percent bracket. Assume you also have a $2,000 balance on your Execucard, which is charging 18 percent interest. That means you're paying $360 a year (with no tax break) to service your debt. The bottom line: You're spending $244.74 a year more than you're making. Even a savings and loan officer can tell you that doesn't make any sense.

Pay off your most expensive debt first. Unless you're swimming with loan sharks, this will be your credit card debt. Think of it this way: Simply by paying off your credit cards, you "earn" 18 percent to 20 percent risk free annually.

Cut up unnecessary cards, then begin paying your monthly bill in full. If you must make installment payments for a large purchase, set up a tight repayment schedule. Never pay the bare minimum—or debt will soon be circling again.

Avoid debt consolidation loans. It's not just that their higher interest rates make them bad deals. Most families wind up owing money again on their credit cards within six months.

By refinancing your mortgage at a lower interest rate, you can slash your monthly payments. For example, let's say you've been paying 11 percent on a fixed-rate, thirty-year loan, and you still owe $80,000. If rates have fallen to 9 percent, you could lower your payments by more than $118 a month, from $761.86 to $643.70. Write yourself a check for the difference each month, and deposit it in savings. As a rule, refinancing makes sense only if current rates are at least two percentage points below yours and you plan to keep your home for another four years. Otherwise any savings will be eaten up by loan fees.

Prepaying principal on your home mortgage can save tens of thousands of dollars in interest (see chapter 5).

Don't hurry to repay low-interest loans, such as student loans, or fixed-rate mortgages, which give you the advantage whether rates are falling (you can refinance) or rising (the joke's on the bank).

■ **Leverage.** Not all debt is evil. Instead of borrowing to buy consumer goods, learn to use credit to build wealth. Temporary borrowing can be a form of forced savings. Sure, you can spend the next five years saving up $10,000 to begin your investing. Or you can borrow $10,000 (at reasonable rates) and start tomorrow. The instant gratification will more than offset the extra interest cost, and the mandatory monthly loan payments are bound to be a more effective prod to saving than a voluntary budget.

The best use of investment leveraging, if one of the most time-consuming, is to buy rental real estate. This income-producing property pays for itself out of rental income. The ideal rental is one with a positive cash flow—that is, one where the rents plus the tax benefits exceed the carrying costs, including interest.

Other good reasons to leverage:

- To fund an IRA or Keogh plan. Your contributions are tax-deductible, even if you don't itemize, while the interest your plan earns is sheltered from tax. These tax benefits, plus your secure retirement, shouldn't be missed because you're short of cash on April 15.

- To start your own business. Like rental real estate, a business has the prospect of paying its own loan interest and principal. Besides, if you fail, why should you lose all of your own savings? The best source of leverage for a business is OPM (other people's money). Finance your venture by rounding up investors to contribute capital in exchange for a share of future profits.

■ **Resist sales pitches.** A silver tongue can make Death Valley sound like the Riviera. But even if a pitch is legitimate, show some mettle. If the pitch is unsolicited, you certainly don't need the product. If you initiated the call, don't be pressured into an immediate decision. Insist on a three-day cooling-off period before committing yourself. Don't buy unless the product still sings a siren song at the end of that time.

Chapter 8

Fast-Track Financial Professionals

Like soybeans, time is a commodity. Don't expect to find it listed on the Chicago Board of Trade, though. Time has its own marketplace—the world of personal service. If you have the money, someone has the time. Time to cook your supper, walk your dog, mow your lawn. Time to help organize your closets or buy your clothes. And most important, time to manage your money, give legal advice, plan your estate, and prepare your tax return.

If you're so busy that your money is a victim of neglect, then buying the time of financial advisers may be your best investment.

Which advisers do you need? That depends on your income, your net worth, the value of your time, and the complexity of your financial affairs. At one time or another almost everyone needs an insurance agent, a tax adviser, or a lawyer (if only to draft a will). On the other hand, if your holdings are limited to a passbook savings account, EE savings bonds, or no-load mutual funds, you can definitely get by without a stockbroker or a money manager. Even if your eye is on Wall Street, you don't need to hire a full-service broker if you have the savvy to make your own stock picks. A simple phone call to a discount broker will do the trick.

When it comes to financial planners, need is less important than affordability. You probably shouldn't hire a financial planner until your earnings are at least $50,000 and your net worth is at least $100,000. The planner's fees will offset the economic benefit of his advice if your wallet weighs less than that.

If you have unique business or investment interests, you may need specialized talent. If you collect art or antiques, for example, you may want an appraiser; if you're an inventor, you need a patent attorney.

Deciding which kind of adviser is right for you is a small step. The near impossible leap is picking the best. There are more advisers than extras in *Ben Hur*. Many are well-trained professionals, but even more are self-styled experts with doubtful credentials, not to mention the outright con artists and frauds.

How can you choose top-notch advisers? One of the most reliable ways is word of mouth. Ask friends, relatives, your employer, or business associates in similar financial circumstances for recommendations. Ask for referrals from professional organizations or the financial advisers you already use.

Make a list of candidates and screen them by phone. Weed out advisers with less than five years' experience, who show little or no interest in your problems, or whose temperament doesn't match yours. Once you've narrowed your prospects to two or three, arrange a face-to-face meeting. Be sure to ask whether there's a fee for this preliminary meeting. If so, decide whether you're willing to pay for it.

The interview usually lasts fifteen to twenty minutes, so be prepared. Know exactly what questions you want to ask, and don't waste time on chitchat.

What are you looking for? Besides such basics as credentials and fees, you're looking for such personal qualities as a reputation for integrity, an understanding of your needs, and a belief that every client is important.

The questions you ask depend in part on the type of advice you're seeking—legal, financial, or tax. But there are some questions you should ask *any* adviser or firm with whom you plan to do business:

- **How long have you (or your firm) been in business?**
- **How large is the firm, and in what areas does it specialize?**
- **What credentials do you have? Do you belong to any professional organizations?** Spot-check his résumé to verify his background.
- **What type of clientele does your firm represent—companies or individuals, large or small portfolios? Are you experienced with clients in circumstances similar to mine?**
- **Are you willing to work with my other advisers?**
- **How are fees charged?** The answer will vary with the type of professional. Lawyers and accountants, for example, charge by the hour. In addition, lawyers normally ask for a retainer if they will be performing frequent or continuing services. Tax preparers, on the other hand, usually charge a flat fee for each tax return, the amount depending upon the number and complexity of the schedules you need. Stockbrokers, insurance agents, and most financial planners receive commissions from products they sell you. If you deal with a commissioned adviser, ask him what he would earn on every investment vehicle he recommends. Ask all ad-

visers whether fees and commissions are negotiable. If the fees seem too high, say so.

■ **Will our agreement and estimated fees be put in writing?**

If the adviser is reluctant to answer such questions or gives you vague or confusing answers, scratch him from your list.

Ask each candidate for the names and phone numbers of three long-standing clients. Make time to call them and ask how the adviser has handled their business—can they reach him quickly when they need to, does he return phone calls promptly, is work done timely, and how much does he charge?

If you've selected more than one adviser, encourage them to work together. Your stockbroker, for example, should consult your tax adviser about the impact of rolling over IRA accounts. If you are planning your estate, your lawyer should speak with your accountant before drawing up wills and trusts. If your team is large, let your financial planner act as coordinator. A major advantage of such teamwork is that it serves as a system of checks and balances, protecting you from out-of-date, inaccurate, or self-serving advice.

No matter how brilliant or trustworthy your advisers, *never* surrender complete control of your finances. No one cares as much about your money as you do. Besides, your lack of interest or awareness makes you an easy mark for advisers who have their commissions, instead of your interests, at heart.

The only way to tell whether you've chosen wisely is to review your advisers' performance. Monitor work carefully for the first few months, then at set intervals. The most important measure is an adviser's success at meeting the goals for which he was hired. Other criteria include timeliness, the level of service, how well you're kept informed, and the professional appearance of correspondence and reports. If you're dissatisfied, find a new adviser.

BANKER

The question these days is not so much where to bank as whether you need a bank at all. Traditional bank services are now offered by credit unions, brokerage firms, finance companies, money market funds, and even such retail chains as Sears.

It pays, therefore, to see whether you can get the same service—or better—elsewhere at lower cost. This especially makes sense with big-ticket items like mortgages, car loans, and investments such as CDs, annuities, and mutual funds. The only areas where banks still hold a shaky lead are number of locations, basic checking, and small-business loans.

When choosing a bank, compare three basic features: safety, convenience, and the value of services. Look for a bank with which you can establish a long and friendly relationship.

It pays to comparison shop for a bank that meets your needs at low cost or no charge. Smaller, community-based banks are often more eager to accommodate customers, especially if they've just opened.

You're more likely to receive special treatment if you bank where your employer, business colleagues, or family bank. Ask your boss, accountant, or relative for a personal introduction to the branch manager or other senior bank officer, or ask them to write a letter of recommendation.

Visit the bank manager from time to time to discuss your banking needs. Cultivating a relationship with a high-level bank employee is the best way to enjoy red-carpet treatment.

During your first chat with the bank officer, ask the following:

- Is there a branch near my home or office?
- What are the bank's hours? Is it open on weekends or until 6 P.M.?
- When's the best time of day to visit the bank for speedy service?
- Is there an express line for simple deposits and withdrawals?
- Can I schedule an appointment to open my account or pick up traveler's checks?
- Can I make deposits by mail? Do you arrange messenger pickup?
- Are your automatic teller machines (ATMs) available twenty-four hours a day? Can I use them to deposit checks and transfer funds? Are ATM transactions free? Is your ATM part of a network such as Cirrus, Star, or TYME? Are there at least two machines at each ATM location in case one breaks down or runs out of money? Is there a service phone near the machines for use when the bank is closed? Are the machines in well-lighted places with video cameras in plain view for security?
- Do you offer home banking by computer? What's the cost? What transactions can be handled electronically? What are the home banking hours? Is a customer service representative available by telephone?
- Is the bank a member of the Federal Deposit Insurance Corporation (FDIC) or the Federal Savings and Loan Insurance Corporation (FSLIC)?
- What range of financial products do you offer—for example, pension plans, discount brokerage, student loans, insurance, a trust and estate department?
- What do you have to offer, considering my specific needs?

For checking accounts:

- **What are your fees?** At most banks, you pay for even the most mundane services. More and more banks, for example, are charging monthly service charges and in some cases per-check charges on checking accounts, ATM transaction fees, and IRA custodial fees. Every stop payment order, money order, certified check, and bounced check (whether you wrote it or received it) also takes a nick out of your funds.
- **Is there a minimum amount I must maintain to avoid these fees or qualify for free services?**
- **Do you offer "bundled" accounts?** Many banks throw in perks for customers who keep high combined balances in checking and savings accounts, CDs, and IRAs. Some let customers who don't meet the minimum requirements pay a monthly fee for these privileges.

Special treatment can include free checking, no- or low-fee and low-interest credit cards, reduced loan rates and mortgage fees, special express lines to teller windows, free twenty-four-hour banking at a network of ATMs nationwide, free safety deposit boxes and personalized checks, no-fee traveler's checks and money orders, and buyer's warranty protection.

With a minimum balance in the six figures, you may be wooed by a combination of banking, discount brokerage, and investment advisory services, which include free checking on interest-bearing accounts, a free gold debit card, a line of credit, a personal account executive, a detailed monthly statement that includes tax totals, and automatic payment of your regular bills.

Although you could probably find better deals on each individual feature of a bundled account by using different banks, the convenience and benefits of a bundle can outweigh the extra cost. All your banking paperwork comes to you on a single statement, you establish a solid banking relationship that could pay off in privileged treatment over time, and you receive a variety of services.

- **Is the monthly statement easy to read? Does the bank return canceled checks?**

For interest-bearing accounts:

- **What's the current interest rate?**
- **How is interest computed?** The ideal account compounds and credits interest daily (or "continuously") from the date of deposit to the day of withdrawal.
- **Is the number of withdrawals per month limited?**
- **Can I write checks on the account?**

For credit cards:

- **What's the annual percentage rate and annual fee?**
- **What's the grace period?** Most banks don't charge interest on your balance for at least twenty-five days after you make a purchase, but a disquieting trend is toward charging from the day of purchase. That means you'll be hit with a finance charge even if you pay off your balance promptly.

PERSONAL BANKER

Increasingly, banks are encouraging a one-on-one relationship with a bank staff member. You're assigned your own personal banker, who will open your accounts, make all loans, and generally handle all non-routine business transactions. This can result in a substantial savings of time and money.

Note that a few snooty, old-money banks won't admit

you into their exclusive club unless you deposit at least $250,000. Others offer personal banking to every customer who opens an account.

How appealing is the bank's promise to grant you a personal banker? Find out by asking the following:

- **How many other clients does my personal banker serve?** The answer should be less than one hundred.
- **Does my personal banker have his own office?** You don't want to discuss your finances at the customer service counter.
- **Can I deal with my personal banker over the telephone?** To a time-strapped investor, not having to meet face to face is invaluable.
- **How knowledgeable is the staffer? Can he explain simply how interest compounds on your certificate of deposit, for example?**

STOCKBROKER

Many people expect their brokers to be a combination of seer, saint, and crystal ball gazer. They're likely to be disappointed. The most a full-service broker can do is offer advice about strategies and recommend promising securities. His tips won't necessarily make you rich.

The best reason to invest through a full-service broker is for sound advice about stocks and bonds. Unfortunately, however, brokers are torn by opposing desires. Although your broker wants his stock picks to add to your wealth, he also wants your stock trading to increase his commissions. You, therefore, have to approach a broker with a mixture of faith and distrust.

Of course, if you can scrounge up enough time and confidence to research your own stocks, you can avoid any conflict of interest by using a discount brokerage firm such as Charles Schwab, Rose & Co., or Quick &

Reilly. Because discounters merely execute trades, you save up to 70 percent if you're buying or selling five hundred shares or more. There are no savings on trades of one hundred shares or less, however, because discounters charge a minimum fee per order.

If you can't devote time to research or simply want advice and camaraderie, then a full-service broker is for you. Look for a firm that's been in business at least ten years, is a member of the New York Stock Exchange, and belongs to the Securities Investor Protection Corporation (SIPC), which insures accounts for up to $500,000 if a brokerage fails (including a maximum of $100,000 in cash).

Select at least three firms and set up a brief meeting with the branch manager to explain your investment needs. Tell the manager how much you have to invest and your goals—for example, you want to invest your $10,000 IRA for retirement and another $10,000 for your toddler's college education. Then ask the manager to recommend a suitable broker if you haven't been referred to a specific individual.

In your interview with the broker, ask the following:

- **When did you become a broker?** The more bear and bull markets the broker has weathered, the more expert he'll be at recognizing and responding to the next up- or downturn.
- **What's your investment approach?** Does his philosophy make sense, and, more important, does it agree with yours? For example, if the broker says "I put all my clients into small-growth stocks" and you prefer blue chips, continue your search.
- **What investment products do you specialize in?** These should be appropriate for your income and match your tolerance for risk. Be leery of investments that are wildly speculative, such as penny stocks, commodities,

and options, or those that carry high commissions or fees, such as closed-end mutual funds, gold, and real estate limited partnerships.

- **Do you do your own research or rely solely on analysts?**
- **Do you own the stocks on your buy list?**
- **What stocks have you bought recently, and why? Will you show me your account statement?** Look for a broker whose answers are logical and consistent with his stated investment approach.
- **What are your firm's commission rates?** The normal rate is 1 percent of the principal. **Do you discount commissions for good customers?**
- **What other fees does your firm charge? Are there processing and handling fees, charges for sending out stock certificates, levies on inactive accounts?**
- **Does your firm offer an asset management account?** (See chapter 5, page 89, for more on this smart money shortcut.) **What other proprietary products and servicesdoes your firm offer?** Some firms, like Merrill Lynch, are virtually financial malls, a selling point for the busy investor.

After the interview, verify the broker's credentials. He should be registered with the National Association of Securities Dealers. Check this out by calling your state securities commission—for the number, call the North American Securities Administrators hot line at 800-942-9022. Ask to be read the broker's CRD file—the Central Registration Depository report the broker must complete. This file tells how long a broker has been in business, where he has worked and for how long, and whether disciplinary actions have ever been brought against him.

If you are suspicious, you can obtain a record of any federal complaints from the SEC's Freedom of Information Branch (450 Fifth St. NW, Mail Stop 2-6, Washington, D.C. 20549).

When you decide where to open an account, give your broker a written list of goals and update them periodically. Be specific. Make it plain that you're interested only in utility stocks, for example. Then, if your broker involves you in oil stocks, he can't claim a lack of communication.

Insist on a certain level of performance. Make sure the broker knows the rate of return or appreciation you expect. This gives him something to strive for besides commissions.

Stress that you want to be alerted not only when to buy, but when to sell—either after the stock has hit a targeted level or after an initial drop in order to prevent further losses. If your portfolio is well diversified, request at least a quarterly performance review.

Never tell the broker, "I don't have time to deal with this. I want you to handle everything." No matter how true it is.

Unless you intend to use it, turn down a margin account, which lets you borrow from your broker to buy stock. Losses on these accounts can be more than ten times your initial investment. Invest a small sum until the broker proves himself.

Don't open a discretionary account, giving your broker authority to make trades without your knowledge or consent. Always take time to confirm in a letter to your broker any instructions or approvals you give by phone.

Finally, check monthly statements and confirmations of trades for accuracy—don't strut around boasting that you never open the envelopes. Contact your broker right away about any questionable items, or you may lose your legal right to damages.

Evaluate your broker's performance after the first six

months and every three months thereafter. Use the prevailing rate of one-year T-bills for comparison. This rate is published in your daily newspaper every Tuesday. If you're not topping it—especially if you're taking high risks—you may want to look for another broker. Be fair, though. If the market crashed again in October, don't blame the decline on your broker.

Look out for certain danger signs:

- Your broker continually pushes securities his firm is underwriting.
- Your broker is constantly on the move from firm to firm.
- You have to earn 10 percent to 12 percent on your investments just to pay the broker's commissions, and the stocks in your account turn over six times in a year (evidence of churning—that is, trading excessively to boost the broker's commissions).

LAWYER

Law touches every area of finance, from loans to taxes to wills. For this reason you may need to hire more than one lawyer—one for real estate transactions, another for business ventures, and a third for estate planning.

You have plenty of choices—a full two-thirds of the world's attorneys, some 750,000, now practice in the United States. In fact, we have more lawyers per person than any other country. But first weigh the cost of a lawyer against the amount of time it would take for you to handle the matter yourself. Law is largely paperwork. If you want to save money instead of time, you may be able to solve your problem by

- filing a complaint with a federal or state consumer protection agency.

- using a legal form or preprinted contract (available from state bar associations and at stationery stores).
- consulting a do-it-yourself legal guidebook. Check the publication date to make sure the book isn't more than two years old. Reputable publishers include Nolo Press and HALT (Help Abolish Legal Tyranny). For an easy-to-read consumer guide, *You and the Law*, call the American Bar Association at 312-988-5000. This 608-page manual sells for $19.98.
- using a computer software program, such as Home Lawyer (Overdrive Systems, $69.95) or Personal Lawyer (BLOC Publishing, $59.95).
- hiring a lawyer for an hour to advise you on alternatives.
- negotiating a compromise yourself.
- seeking arbitration or mediation.
- taking your case to small claims court.

When is a lawyer necessary? Obviously, no matter how minor your legal problem, you need a lawyer if you don't have time to deal with it yourself. In addition, always seek the services of a skilled general practitioner or specialist if you need help establishing a small business, signing a contract for a large sum of money, arranging a tax-deferred exchange, resolving estate or tax problems involving substantial amounts of money or property, or preparing a will or living trust.

Even if you need professional help, most legal matters are routine enough to be handled by a legal clinic or an inexpensive legal chain, such as Jacoby & Meyers or Hyatt Legal Services. Fees are usually 10 percent to 50 percent below those charged by private practitioners.

If you want a specialist, don't pay extra for the prestige of a big-name firm. Those partnerships charge up to $350 an hour. If you can't get a referral from a friend or relative, contact your state or local bar association for the names of small firms or sole practitioners who handle your type of case. You can also check the Yellow Pages for specialties and locations.

Your employer or union may offer a prepaid legal plan as a fringe benefit. For a flat annual fee of between $100 and $200, you have unlimited use of the group's lawyers for simple tasks, such as reviewing contracts. You receive a discount of up to 30 percent on a lawyer's hourly rate for more complicated cases.

When investigating prospective lawyers, ask the following questions:

- **What percentage of your practice is devoted to cases like mine?** Ask about the results of similar cases, including time spent and fees charged.
- **Will you personally work on my case or delegate it to an associate?** If your case will be handled by an associate, will his services be billed separately at his lower rate? Take time to meet the associate at the end of the interview.
- **How long will it take to complete the case, and what's your estimate of the cost?** When you retain a lawyer, request a timetable of actions and the approximate date they'll be completed. Ask to be kept informed of every development in the case—even the fact that there are no developments.
- **Do you base your charges on "minimum billing units?"** For example, if your attorney's minimum billing unit is fifteen minutes, you'll be charged for that much time if he so much as writes a memo or answers a phone call from you, even if it takes less than five minutes.
- **If you and I disagree, will you consent to binding arbitration?** This can save you a tremendous amount of legal fees in the event of a dispute.

Have your lawyer draw up a written retainer agreement. It should include the following:

- All agreed-upon services. For example, will he write letters presenting your demands? Will he represent you in court?
- The hourly rate. How much is the initial retainer? Hold out for a "deductible retainer," in which your lawyer's hourly charges are subtracted from the money you pay up front. For example, if your lawyer charges $150 per hour and the deductible retainer is $900, based on an estimate of the amount of work involved, you're entitled to six hours of legal work before his meter starts running. If he won't agree to this arrangement, find another lawyer.
- A written estimate of all costs, including expenses.
- How often you wish to be billed.
- How often, on what issues, and in what form the lawyer will communicate with you. For example, will he call you every two weeks or just when there's a new development?
- A provision for settling any disputes, such as fee disagreements.

Ask that all bills be itemized and sent to you regularly. You may also want to set a ceiling on costs, which can be exceeded only with your written permission.

To make the most efficient, least expensive use of your lawyer's time:

- Write down questions and important points before meetings. Use self-help legal guides to help you formulate questions and assemble the information your lawyer needs in advance.
- Bring in every document, whether it seems relevant or not.

- Tell your lawyer the whole truth, even if some of it is harmful to your case.
- Don't use your lawyer as a marriage counselor, psychiatrist, or investment adviser.

TAX PRACTITIONER

Most people would rather face Jaws than Form 1040. This fear isn't helped any by Congress, which unleashes "reform" every time you think it's safe to go back into the tax law.

If you can conquer your fears, however, you may discover you can handle your taxes alone—as do some fourteen million Americans who itemize. You can probably prepare your return yourself if

- your income is mainly from wages.
- your write-offs are limited to the most common itemized deductions (medical expense, interest, contributions, or taxes).
- you don't own rental property, your own business, or limited partnership interests.
- you don't sell your home or other investment property during the year.

If you want to file solo, buy an up-to-date tax guide, such as *The Money Income Tax Handbook* by Mary L. Sprouse. You may also want to call your local IRS office for a copy of its free Publication 17, *Your Federal Income Tax* (look in the White Pages under "U.S. Government"). If you own a computer, consider one of the tax software programs discussed in chapter 9.

If you decide to use a tax professional, you have four categories to choose from: certified public accountants (CPAs), attorneys, enrolled agents, and unenrolled tax preparers.

CERTIFIED PUBLIC ACCOUNTANT (CPA)

A certified public accountant must have a college degree, pass a four-part national exam in accounting, and take annual college-level refresher courses. He could probably audit General Motors blindfolded. Does he know anything about taxes? Not necessarily. Like doctors, CPAs specialize. Make sure yours specializes in taxes.

Do you really need such a tax thoroughbred? If you're self-employed, the answer is probably yes. The same is true if you're about to be divorced, retire, or move to a different state; you expect an inheritance; you own tax shelters or other tax-advantaged investments; or you'd benefit significantly from tax planning—generally if you're in the highest tax bracket with an annual income of $60,000 or more.

Don't go big-name hunting: the large firms cater to corporate clients. Hire an accountant with a small firm or in private practice instead. Expect to pay from $250 to $500 for your return.

TAX ATTORNEY

A tax attorney has specialized legal training and experience and therefore should be more knowledgeable about the tax law than other preparers lacking these credentials. But tax attorneys rarely prepare tax returns. Instead they hand out advice on such complicated tax issues as estate planning, foreign taxes, partnership taxation, or divorce. They also represent clients being pursued or prosecuted by the IRS.

Attorneys are costly, charging from $125 to $275 an hour and up, depending on the complexity of the tax issue and the size of the firm.

When should you consult a tax attorney? When

you're in the clutches of the IRS, be it an audit, tax lien, or criminal investigation. When large sums of money are about to change hands, for example, when you're buying real estate, selling a business, or getting a divorce. When you want advice about the best form of doing business—as a sole proprietor, partnership, or regular or S corporation—in order to minimize taxes and limit your liability.

ENROLLED AGENTS

Few taxpayers have ever heard of enrolled agents, but these tax experts are generally excellent preparers. They have won their credentials by passing a grueling two-day examination given by the IRS. Others have served at least five years with the Internal Revenue Service at the auditor level or higher. Enrolled agents who are members of the National Association of Enrolled Agents must also take at least thirty hours of class work in tax matters each year.

In an audit, an enrolled agent has the same status as an attorney or CPA, being authorized to practice before the IRS and represent you at the appellate level if your audit is appealed.

Although an enrolled agent often provides the same quality of tax preparation and planning as an attorney or CPA, he does so at 25 percent less cost.

There are roughly 28,000 enrolled agents in active practice. To locate an enrolled agent in your area, call the National Association of Enrolled Agents at 800-424-4339.

UNENROLLED AGENTS

Finally, there are unenrolled tax preparers. I mention this category because a large percentage of preparers are unenrolled, but I don't recommend their services. Most of these preparers work part-time for tax preparation chains, such as H & R Block and Triple Check, or other storefront operations.

In most states, an unenrolled tax preparer has no formal qualifications. For this reason exercise extreme caution if you decide to select such a preparer. Many unenrolled preparers are retired persons or workers in other fields who moonlight during the tax season. Their tax training is usually haphazard at best, although H & R Block preparers must complete the firm's eighty-one-hour, $195 tax course and, if hired, attend a forty-hour refresher course each year.

If you have a simple return, an unenrolled preparer does offer two advantages: speed and reasonable fees. Your return is usually completed in one or two days. The fee for a short form is usually around $50; a Form 1040 with itemized deductions averages around $100. This buys you tax preparation, but no tax planning advice.

PICK OR PASS?

No matter which category of preparer you choose, start early. Meet with two or three practitioners at the beginning of January. Take along your tax returns for the past two years, plus an estimate of your current year's income and expenses.

Address any specific concerns—will you be subject to alternative minimum tax, for example—and ask what additional deductions you may be able to take. Pay particular attention to *how* the preparer answers. Are his responses clear and complete? Even if an answer is no, does he explain why? Pass up any preparer who tells you "The law is too complex, you won't understand it."

While you're at it, also ask these questions:

- **How much will it cost to prepare the return?** If the preparer quotes a flat fee, find out what, if anything, is included besides return preparation. What does he charge for tax planning or technical advice after the filing season?

- **How many 1040s do you prepare annually? How many returns did you prepare on extension last year?** Unless his practice involves mostly short forms, a preparer would be hard-pressed to competently handle more than four hundred returns a year without assistance. Practitioners who file extensions for more than 15 percent of their clients may be stretching themselves too thin. The probable result: delay in completing your return, unreturned phone calls, and little or no tax planning advice.

- **How do you keep current on changes in the tax law?** He should either subscribe to tax newsletters, keep an up-to-date set of tax books, or take continuing education classes.

- **Will you represent me if I'm audited? What's the extra cost for this service?**

- **Will you pay interest and penalties levied as a result of errors on the return?**

- **Are you conservative or aggressive in your tax philosophy?** This key question decides compatibility. If you want all the deductions you have coming, even at the risk of an audit, say so. Otherwise your preparer may tiptoe too cautiously around the IRS to avoid losing you as a client. If you're uncomfortable testing the law's gray areas, make that plain, too.

Beware of the preparer who

- sets up shop in January, then closes his doors in April. Tax problems can occur at any time of the year. Make sure the preparer will be around if you're audited or queried by the IRS.

- guarantees you a refund or whose fee is a percentage of your refund.
- promises "no audit." The IRS randomly selects thousands of returns for audit based on computer formulas, and no one can guarantee yours won't be among them.
- makes questionable suggestions, such as that you overlook an item of income, or takes little or no time to find out the facts. A good preparer explains the law or gives you helpful hints to improve your record keeping or tax situation.
- asks you to sign a blank return. Always demand a copy of your return. And never allow the preparer to use his address on the top of the return so that your refund comes to him.

To ensure accuracy you must personally review your return thoroughly before signing. Don't be afraid to question items you don't understand, and insist on clear, convincing answers. Remember, the IRS holds you responsible for any mistakes on the return, no matter who prepares it.

Don't think of tax preparation as an annual event. Meet with your adviser in May or June to go over your taxes in more detail and to discuss long-range strategies. Call before making major decisions, such as buying or selling a house, making a large charitable contribution, or setting up a custodian account for your child.

INSURANCE AGENT

In chapter 2, I advised consolidating your insurance policies under one roof for maximum time savings. That means choosing just one agent to handle all your insurance needs. However, because agents specialize, this may not be entirely possible. You may find one agent who's terrific for life, health, and disability insurance and another who's a whiz at property and casualty policies (home, auto, and so on).

Agents come in two varieties—those who represent just one company, called captive agents or direct writers, and independent agents who work for different insurers, usually five or more.

An independent agent has the advantage of choice. If a product offered by one company doesn't fit your finances, an independent agent has an array of other products to offer. A captive agent, on the other hand, can sell only his company's product, even if it's wrong for you.

Nevertheless, a captive agent may offer the best rates or service in certain areas.

Ultimately your choice should be based on price and your sense of the agent's integrity and competence.

Here are some suggested interview questions:

- **How long have you been an agent?** The mortality rate among insurance agents is alarming. According to Rebekah S. Verdon of Ken Ulis & Company, a Los Angeles insurance firm, of every one hundred agents hired, only five will be left at the end of one year and just one will remain after five years. If yours doesn't have five years' experience, therefore, his office may be a doughnut shop the next time you stop by.
- **What are your professional credentials?** A chartered life underwriter (CLU) or chartered property/casualty underwriter (CPCU) has spent considerable time acquiring a solid working knowledge of insurance and has passed a series of tough exams.

- **How do you keep up to date on the latest insurance legislation, tax law changes, and products?** Although there is no continuing education requirement, your agent should attend courses and seminars throughout the year.
- **Do you carry malpractice insurance?**
- **What's the quality of the companies you represent?** Most or all of them should be rated A+ in *Best's Insurance Reports,* and at least 90 percent of them should be licensed in New York. Because New York State's insurance laws are the toughest in the nation, many companies stay out; otherwise they'd have to conform to New York's strict standards *nationwide.* Instead they set up subsidiaries to do business in New York.

By the same token, be wary of agents who peddle products of insurance companies based in Texas, where standards are lax.

- **How much are the premiums on the amount and type of coverage I need?** Consult your financial planner about your insurance needs beforehand or explain your financial situation to the agent during the interview.
- **Do I qualify for any discounts?**
- **How does the policy you suggest fit my needs?**
- **What's the cost index of the policy you recommend?** The cost index is a special number developed to facilitate comparison shopping for insurance and reflects the price of the policy. The lower the index number, the better the bargain. Use this number to compare similar term, whole-life, and universal-life policies.
- **Who will handle any property or casualty claim?** There's no "right" answer—this is merely for your information. Independent agents normally deal with the matter themselves. If you use a direct writer, claims are usually processed by the insurance company's claims department.

- **How often will you be in touch with me to review my coverage?** Your agent should check back with you at least once a year.

Also consider the following:

- Are the agent's explanations of price, amount of coverage, and policy benefits clear and specific?
- Does he ask what insurance coverage your employer provides in order to prevent duplication?
- Is he a high-pressure salesman? Does he try to shame or alarm you into buying coverage you don't want or need? Does he try to sell you a high-commission whole-life policy when all you want is term insurance?
- Is he willing to make three or four visits to sell you a policy, or does he demand an immediate decision?
- Does he offer products that seem too good to be true—you know better, don't you?

To do a background check, contact your state insurance commission for a record of any disbarment. Then hope your agent didn't chalk up a bad record in another state.

Of course, there's a chance you don't need an agent. If you already know what kind of insurance you need and how much, you can save considerable time by buying from a company that sells by telephone and mail. These include Colonial Penn (800-523-1919) Amica Mutual, which sells primarily home and auto insurance (800-242-6422), and USAA, which specializes in life and disability policies (800-531-8000).

FINANCIAL PLANNER

Think of your finances as a set of scales that must be delicately balanced. If you invest too heavily on the side of tax savings, favoring low income and deductions over higher income and appreciation, for example, your retirement fund will be underweight, or you'll be light on tuition when your namesake heads for college. If you put too much money into stocks, the scales may tip dangerously if the market plummets.

You can attempt this balancing act yourself, or you can hire a financial planner. One reason to use a financial planner is the reason you're reading this book—you're too busy to make the most of your money. Or you lack the desire to keep up with today's wide variety of investment choices, our ever-changing tax law, and the complexities of your employer's compensation and benefit programs. Or maybe you need encouragement and structure to save.

Your net worth and income are also important factors. There's no point considering a full financial plan until your family income or your investable assets exceed $50,000. Below that, the cost of hiring a planner—$500 to $5,000 in the first year—outweighs the economic benefit.

What if you want help only with a special problem? Suppose you inherit money, a parent needs long-term nursing care, or you changed jobs and took a lump-sum distribution from your retirement plan. Many financial planners will give you advice on a single issue for a flat fee.

What is a financial planner? A financial planner is a master of the pie chart—advising you to put X percent of your money in term life insurance and Y percent in mutual funds, for instance. He makes sure all the elements—cash flow, debts, taxes, retirement, estate planning, and insurance—remain balanced. He also sees to it that your investments are well diversified, to keep your yield steady if the economy falters.

A planner drafts a written plan suggesting alternative investments to meet your specific goals. A budget may also be included to help you save needed capital. Finally, you receive estate planning advice.

Acting on this plan is up to you, however. Some people treat their plans like menus, following advice only when it agrees with decisions they've already made. Others shut theirs in a drawer and forget about them. The financial plan is a blueprint; you must be the builder.

Proceed with caution, however, because anyone can call himself a financial planner. More than a hundred thousand do. Only one in three is qualified. Many are outright con men.

This is bad news for time-strapped investors. It means each candidate must be rigorously investigated. But cutting short the selection process would be foolhardy. With no regulatory body overseeing the industry, there are plenty of scoundrels eager for your money.

How can you choose a trustworthy planner? Be diligent about asking the following questions:

- **What's your education and experience?** Verify his impressive list of degrees.
- **Are you licensed by the state to sell securities or insurance?** Many self-styled planners are stockbrokers or insurance agents in disguise. In that case, what you think is objective advice may be nothing more than a way to sell a single product.
- **Are you or your firm registered with the Securities and Exchange Commission?** If not, why? Ask to see the ADV form that financial planners or their firms must file

with the SEC. This states the planner's experience, how he is paid, whether he has a financial interest in the investments he sells, and whether he has been disciplined by regulatory agencies. You can also get copies of this form from Bechtel Information Technology's SEC Express (800-231-3282) or Disclosure Inc. (800-638-8241).

It's also a good idea to check with the securities regulator in the state where the adviser practices.

A quick check: Call the Financial Planning Resource Foundation (900-786-7237). For $2 per minute, you can find out whether the planner has been reprimanded by the SEC or other regulators.

- **What are your professional credentials?** A certified financial planner (CFP) or a chartered financial consultant (Ch.FC) must pass a series of exams and have three or more years of experience. A registered financial planner (RFP) has passed state insurance and securities exams. Other initials that may be listed after a planner's name are CFA (chartered financial analyst), MSFS (master of science in financial services), and the more easily recognized CPA, MBA, and JD (law degree).

If he's a fee-only planner, he should be a member of the National Association of Personal Financial Advisors. Write to the NAPFA, 1130 Lake Cook Road, Suite 105, Buffalo Grove, IL 60089, for a directory of members in your region.

If you demand the best, interview only members of the Registry of Financial Planning Practitioners. For a free list of registry members, write to the IAFP, 2 Concourse Pkwy., Suite 800, Atlanta, GA 30328.

- **How are you compensated?** Cross off "commission only" planners. Their advice is free because they earn their living from commissions on investments and insurance they sell you. They may be sorely tempted to push products you don't need.

"Fee only" planners don't sell anything. They charge a flat fee, hourly fee, or percentage fee for their advice, your annual plan, and any periodic reviews. Fee-only planners are much more likely to solve problems using no- or low-cost techniques or investments. For example, they may recommend a Keogh plan to save you taxes rather than a high-commission tax shelter.

This objectivity doesn't come cheap. Expect to pay a fee-only planner from $1,500 to $5,000 in the first year and about half that in subsequent years. For this reason many clients of fee-only planners have incomes of at least $100,000.

If your income is between $50,000 and $100,000, a "fee-and-commission" planner is more economical, with costs topping out at about $600 for the first year. Just remember that these planners are also salespeople—60 percent to 80 percent of their incomes is from commissions. You therefore have a right to ask your planner to justify his investment choices.

Some fee-and-commission planners offer the option of selecting your own investments or buying the financial products they sell.

- **How much money will you or any member of your firm make on each investment you sell me?**
- **If you receive commissions, roughly what percentage of your firm's commission income derives from insurance products, annuities, mutual funds, limited partnerships, stock and bonds, other?** Watch out for a drastic imbalance, for example, if the firm receives over half of its income from limited partnerships. This indicates the firm is pushing one particular type of investment for profit whether or not it meets a client's needs.
- **Does your service include recommendations for specific investments or investment products?** Some fee-only planners make generic recommendations, such as

growth mutual funds or term life insurance. If you want more concrete guidance, move on to the next candidate.

■ **Do you assist in implementing the plan?** This is a question of convenience and cost. The fee-only planner usually directs you to other specialists, such as an accountant or an attorney, to take action on the plan. This takes up more of your time, plus you'll have to pay the fees of these professionals as well.

A fee-and-commission planner will save you time by helping to implement, but the fee to do so is often excessive.

■ **How will you arrive at your recommendations?** Will the planner personally research and draft a written analysis based on your needs? Or will it be a canned plan derived by feeding your vital statistics into a computer? *Note:* If you'll receive the plan in less than a month, it's probably canned.

Computerized financial plans aren't necessarily bad. They're cheap, and even though they're a plug for the issuing institution's products, you're not obliged to buy. You can take their investment advice elsewhere. These prefab plans aren't recommended for incomes over $75,000, however, since their suggestions assume a smaller amount to invest and do not explore all the options available to the large investor.

■ **What rate of return can I expect in five years?** A planner should outpace inflation by at least 4 percent or 5 percent a year. Beware a guaranteed return well above current market rates, however—such investments may be fraudulent.

■ **Are you willing to work with my other financial advisers when necessary?** He should agree to give each a copy of the relevant portion of your financial plan.

■ **What's your typical client's income?** Your income should be in the same ballpark.

- **May I see a sample plan?** He should be able to give you a copy of a recent plan written for a client with needs similar to your own. The name will be blacked out for confidentiality.
- **Will you provide such ongoing services as updating my plan and periodic reviews?**
- **May I see your last two Forms 1040?** A good planner expects to see your tax returns, so ask the same of him. How he invests his own money will be a clue to what advice he'll give you.

Evaluate your planner a year after you receive the written plan. Have you met your short-term goals? Are you making progress on your long-term goals? Have your investments yielded the desired level of return? Has your net worth increased? Do you feel secure? If so, congratulations. If not, don't hesitate to switch—there's no contract binding you.

MONEY MANAGERS

Like chauffeurs and private jets, money managers are a mark of status and privilege. In the past, that was because most of the best managers wouldn't handle assets of less than $250,000 or $500,000. Even if you find one of the growing number today who will handle individuals with $50,000 or less to invest, the fees can make joining the elite unappealing.

Money managers usually charge an annual fee of 1 percent to 2 percent of your account's assets, with a minimum fee of $800 to $1,000. In addition, you pay the brokerage commissions when your manager trades stocks or bonds on your behalf. These can run from 1 percent to 2 percent of your assets in the first year, when the manager must buy a complete portfolio. In subsequent years they drop about a quarter of a percent. If you have less than $50,000, the combined management fee and commissions could consume up to 4 percent of your holdings. In such cases you can probably do equally well with a good no-load mutual fund—which is run by a specialized money manager.

What services does a money manager provide? Unlike the financial planner, who helps define your financial goals, a manager is an investment specialist who takes complete charge of your portfolio. This makes him the most time-efficient financial professional, bar none. In most cases you sign an agreement permitting him to trade for your account without asking you first. If you can't sleep while a stranger is juggling your nest eggs, a money manager is not for you.

Although the money manager decides which stocks to buy and sell, a broker makes the actual trades. You can use your own broker or one who does business with the money manager. These brokers usually discount their rates from 20 percent to 50 percent, depending on the volume of trading and the size of your account.

The brokerage firm or bank should act as custodian for your account. This keeps a light-fingered money manager from looting your funds.

As you interview each money manager, consider the following:

- **Investment philosophy.** Does the manager excel at putting together income-producing bonds and high-yielding stocks, or does he prefer growth stocks that rack up large capital gains? Does he buy and hold conservatively, or is he an aggressive trader? Does he practice market timing, use a low price-earnings method, or use stock options to hedge his bets?

To ensure that your investment goals mirror the manager's philosophy after you hire him, spell out your guidelines in the client agreement. For example, you might state that your portfolio should outperform rates on long-term certificates of deposit by at least three percentage points, net of all fees, or that you must be consulted before the manager buys over-the-counter stock.

- **Trading history.** Compare the manager's performance year by year with an index found in your library, such as Standard & Poor's 500 Stock Index or, for fixed-income or balanced accounts, the Shearson Treasury Bond Index. Not even first-rate managers can be expected to beat these indexes every year, but they should be able to show superior results—generally a 20 percent or better compound annual rate of return—over a period of five years or more.

Don't fall for the manager with the flashiest track record. There are countless ways to gussy up performance. Each manager can select which kinds of accounts to include in the average, count only the largest account, pick a favorable starting point at the beginning of a bull market, or omit disastrous results.

Beware, too, the manager who uses "model" accounts or arbitrary indexes to report performance. These hypothetical accounts don't exist and are no proof of actual performance. No better is the "representative account" that is actually the manager's best performer.

Ask the manager for a report that reflects a composite of all accounts he has carte blanche to run. Make sure he has deducted his annual fees and trading commissions from the total return.

- **Background.** He should be registered with the Securities and Exchange Commission (SEC), but the standards aren't high. Almost anyone who hasn't been convicted of a felony and can raise the $150 registration fee can be a registered adviser.

Request a copy of the ADV form—short for application for registration as an investment adviser—the manager filed with the SEC. This form discloses the manager's education, experience, fees, and investment strategy. It also reveals whether the manager or firm has been disciplined by the SEC or other regulatory agencies.

You can find money managers at brokerage firms and bank trust departments, although the latter seldom bother with accounts under $500,000. Others work for small, independent, investment advisory firms controlling between $50 million and $500 million. Ask for referrals from your financial planner, broker, or accountant, or check the ads in financial publications and investment newsletters. Remember, in this electronic age there's no need to stick close to home. You don't have time to watch over his shoulder anyway.

Some brokerage firms, such as Shearson Lehman, Dean Witter Reynolds, Paine Webber, Merrill Lynch, and Prudential Securities, play matchmaker and put you in touch with a money manager. The fee is a steep 3 percent, but it covers both the money manager's annual fee and the brokerage's commissions and custodial fees. One selling point is that the manager's performance is monitored by the broker, who assumes fiduciary responsibility. Nevertheless, you may find that the hefty fee and little if any personal contact with the manager are drawbacks.

Evaluate your manager's performance with each quarterly statement. Are the stocks in your portfolio the kinds of companies you'd buy? Ask how they fit in with your objectives. If you have losses, ask the manager to explain them and to tell you what he's doing to correct them. Once a year, review how well your manager has met your goals, how well he did compared to the markets in which your money was invested, and whether you could have done almost as well with a money market or mutual fund.

Chapter 9

High-Tech Financial Help

Want to take a big byte out of the time you spend managing your money? Put the power of the microchip to work for you. Not only can a computer free you from time-consuming tasks, it can increase your profits, too.

A personal computer is an awesome investment tool. It relieves you of menial and repetitive chores, such as manual calculation and record keeping. It manages your budget, figures your taxes, tracks and evaluates any type of investment, reduces risks, and provides instant access to an immense storehouse of financial data. You can buy software to help you pick stocks, mutual funds, bonds, and real estate.

Before you get overexcited, remember that money management takes more than math. A computer may be Einstein, but it's not Solomon. It has no caution, self-discipline, or common sense. It can't pick surefire winners or protect you from a fondness for losers.

In fact, it can't function at all without numbers. That means sitting hunched over your keyboard for several hours or minutes a week. And most software programs take about a day to learn. Don't begrudge the time you have to put in at the beginning. It will more than pay for itself in time savings later on.

Once you decide to automate, a good place to start is with your personal finances. Without money you can't begin to invest.

CASH AND BUDGET MANAGEMENT

Of all the potential uses of your computer, none outweighs managing your cash and budgeting. A computer tracks your assets and maximizes the cash you have to invest by controlling your spending—essential for successful investing.

With personal finance software, you can throw away the shoebox and do bookkeeping handsprings. Double-entry bookkeeping is automatic—if you pay a doctor bill, your checking balance is reduced, and your medical expenses account is increased. You can also split transactions and allocate a payment to several different expense categories (for example, when you pay a credit card bill, you're paying several bills with one check). The result: financial reports that save hours of compilation time, making tax time a lark and budgeting a breeze.

Once you've mastered the basics of the software, monitoring your finances shouldn't take more than half an hour each week.

For sheer speed and ease, you can't beat Quicken (Intuit, $59.95). This program, which is patterned after your everyday checkbook, is as friendly as a wet dog. You can have it up and running in minutes, with virtually all the help you need on-screen. Quicken tracks your cash, checking account, and credit card balances, expenses, and net worth. It also performs simple investment tracking, takes care of small-business and rental bookkeeping, and prints checks, income and expense reports, and a tax summary. At year end your tax data can be exported to Chipsoft's TurboTax, MECA's Tax-Cut, and J. K. Lasser's Your Income Tax Software.

Probably the most comprehensive finance program is Andrew Tobias's Managing Your Money (MECA, $219.98). Besides balancing your checkbook, this program sets up a household budget, estimates your income tax, manages your portfolio, assists with insurance and retirement planning, figures compound interest, and calculates your net worth. Sophisticated investors will appreciate the extra planning features, although the many options make it more time-consuming to learn. You can also import tax information directly into MECA's TaxCut.

Built into both Quicken and Managing Your Money is CheckFree, an electronic bill-paying program. You type in the amount and name of the payee and send it via modem to CheckFree. CheckFree debits your bank account automatically and either prints a check or credits your payee's bank account. The cost of the program is $10 a month. If you don't have Quicken or Managing Your Money, you can buy CheckFree's software for $30 at software stores or directly from CheckFree Corporation (720 Greencrest Drive, Westerville, OH 43081, 800-882-5280).

INVESTMENT EVALUATION AND SELECTION

No function shows off the gee-whiz, time-saving nature of computers better than investing. Your computer can sort through thousands of stocks and sift through millions of statistics in the time it takes you to turn on your adding machine. It can analyze these reams of data and present the result in a format you can understand at a glance. Computerized investing frees you to make investment decisions, instead of wasting time drawing laborious graphs or scouring the pages of *Value Line.*

Your computer lets you apply the same information and theory to building your portfolio that the high-priced money managers use. It also lets you play the valuable game of "What If." For example, you can create several hypothetical portfolios and chart them before actually investing any of your hard-won money. Or you can compare information about different investments to determine which pays the best total return.

By doing the work of your broker, your computer saves on commissions (you can use a discount firm) and assures that buy-sell decisions are based on more objective standards than your broker's desire to earn a commission.

Expect to pay between $200 and $700 for good programs that don't include data feed and up to $2,000 for those with data feed (plus data-base charges).

Because of the cost of investment programs, you might want to seek advice from users first. Look into computerized bulletin boards or user groups. The Boston Computer Society has a library of investment software its members can try out (617-252-0600). The largest network of computer groups for investors is sponsored by the American Association of Individual Investors (312-280-0170). Its annual fee includes a subscription to its bimonthly *Computerized Investing Newsletter* and a directory of user groups, bulletin boards, and software.

Other electronic investment clubs include LinchPin (modem line 617-742-9194), Channel 1 (modem line 617-354-8873), Dollars & Bytes (modem line 619-483-5477), and the Market (modem line 301-299-8667). All are free except Channel 1, which charges an annual fee.

Investment programs offer help on three fronts: technical analysis, fundamental analysis, and portfolio management.

TECHNICAL ANALYSIS

Following a dozen or more securities in various industries, each reacting differently to trends in inflation or interest rates, takes more than pen and paper. Luckily there are many programs on the market that track stocks, bonds, mutual funds, options, and commodities.

These programs analyze market trends. They graph movements in a stock's price and trading volume over time and tell you the best times to buy and sell. A good package plots a huge array of charts and graphs and offers a variety of techniques to analyze price data. You can also plug in prices to test your own hunches and theories.

Among the better technical software packages are

- *MetaStock Professional* (Equis International, 800-882-3040/801-265-8886): This is the best entry-level program for both beginners and sophisticated investors, with windowing capability that lets you put as many as thirty charts on the screen.
- *Telescan Analyzer* (Telescan Inc., 713-952-1060): Best for novice chartists, this program provides fifty benchmarks, including price-to-earnings ratios, on 10,000 stocks and 1,700 mutual funds and displays information in graphs.
- *Market Analyzer Plus* (Dow Jones, 609-520-4642): This program pulls data from Dow Jones News/Retrieval and analyzes trading patterns of stocks, bonds, Treasury issues, mutual funds, and options for a low monthly fee.

- *Wall Street Investor* (Pro Plus Software, 800-227-5728): The Rolls-Royce of investment software for both IBMs and Macs, this menu-driven and easy-to-use program provides portfolio management, technical and fundamental analysis, and on-line trading.

Mutual fund packages include

- *Markex* (Markex Inc., 800-334-7940): A simple program designed for investors with no time or desire to follow their holdings closely, Markex tells you when to stay in or get out of equity funds.
- *Mutual Fund Investor* (American River Software, 916-483-1600): For those who like to check up on their funds every week or so, this program compares your fund's performance graphically with other funds and the Standard & Poor's 500 Stock Index.
- *Investor's FastTrack* (800-749-1348): This program lets you easily follow more than five hundred portfolios on a daily basis, displays price charts for funds you choose, tracks various technical signals, including moving averages, and ranks mutual funds on their current performance and investment potential.
- *Fund Master-TC* (TimeTrend Software, 508-663-3330): Aimed at sophisticated investors and stockbrokers, this software does advanced technical analysis on many funds.

Note: You can print charts showing high prices, low prices, moving averages, and dozens of other technical indicators, but unless you know how to read them, you might as well use them as wallpaper. Two books that teach you how to interpret your data are *Technical Analysis of Stock Trends,* by Robert D. Edwards and John Magee (John Magee Inc., $75), and *Secrets for Profiting in*

Bull and Bear Markets, by Stan Weinstein (Dow Jones–Irwin, $24.95).

FUNDAMENTAL ANALYSIS

With a modem and communications software to connect your computer with a data base, you can also screen securities for any market indicators or other traits, such as debt-to-equity ratios. Stock screening software takes just minutes to search through a data base of thousands of stocks and identify a short, specific list that meets your predefined criteria. Some do only "absolute" screening—finding all stocks, for example, with a price-earnings ratio of less than 10 and a price less than $50 per share. Others let you assign different weights to each factor.

If you're an occasional investor, you should probably subscribe to a pay-as-you-go screening service, such as CompuServe (800-848-8990). This on-line service screens for favorable debt-equity ratios, price-book value, returns on sales, cash flow, and assets and equity. It also compares a stock's current price to past performance or measures a stock's price fluctuations.

If you're a frequent trader, consider more expensive stock-screening services that update information by mailing you disks on a weekly, monthly, or quarterly basis. These include

- *Market Base* (MP Software, 800-735-0700): analyzes 4,600 stocks and screens for the most variables.
- *Value/Screen II* (Value Line, 800-654-0508): uses Value Line ratings to screen 1,600 stocks.
- *Telescan Edge* (Telescan Inc., 713-952-1060): a blend of fundamental and technical analysis, providing data on 10,000 stocks and 1,700 mutual funds.
- *Stockpak II* (Standard & Poor's Corp., 212-208-8581):

screens up to 4,600 stocks, including 2,200 over-the-counter issues, for eighty variables, including Standard & Poor's own ranking of earnings and dividend stability.

- *Stock Market Data Bank* (American Investors Alliance, 305-561-1900): information on 3,500 stocks, plus a letter-writing feature.
- *Compustock* (A. S. Gibson & Sons, 801-298-4578): analyzes price-earnings ratios, dividends, earnings, returns on assets and equity, and inventory turnover for 1,500 stocks.

Mutual fund screening services include

- *Mutual Fund Scoreboard* (Business Week, 800-553-3575): screens 580 equity funds using over twenty variables and ranks according to size, expense ratios, portfolio composition, risk, and *BusinessWeek*'s own fund ratings.
- *Rugg & Steele Mutual Fund Selector* (Rugg & Steele Inc., 800-237-8400, ext. 678/818-340-0179): evaluates 1,250 equity and 1,040 bond funds according to risk and total return, screens for twenty variables, and ranks funds based on various characteristics, such as performance during bear markets.

PORTFOLIO MANAGEMENT

With most portfolio management programs, you can compute the market value of your entire portfolio in a matter of minutes. Simply update prices from newspaper stock tables or via modem from an on-line information service. With each update the software computes the new value of your portfolio. You can even set prices at which you want to sell or buy shares, and your computer will alert you when it's time to act.

The first choice of many investors is the ubiquitous Managing Your Money. This general personal finance program stores and updates up to three hundred stocks or other investments. For simple investment tracking, you can also use Quicken or business spreadsheets, such as Lotus 1-2-3.

If you're monitoring an extensive portfolio, you might need a more powerful product. Most track multiple portfolios, a plus if you want to test your investment theories by speculating with play money. They also compute your profit or loss on sales, taking into account interest, dividends, and commissions—then print a schedule of capital gains or losses at tax time. Schwab's Equalizer lets you trade electronically as well.

Several such portfolio managers include

- *Market Manager Plus* (Dow Jones Software, 609-520-4641): This easy-to-use program, which runs on both IBM and Macs, includes the usual reports on holdings, transactions, and gains or losses, plus it alerts you to maturing bonds and Treasury bills and provides access to Dow Jones/News Retrieval for easy updating of your portfolio.
- *The Equalizer* (Charles Schwab & Co., 800-334-4455): Designed to enable investors to execute trades through Charles Schwab, this program also contains a strong portfolio manager that includes subscriptions to Dow Jones, Warner pricing, and Standard & Poor's MarketScope, at considerably less cost than Market Manager Plus.
- *PFROI* (Techserve, 800-826-8082): No doubt the best bargain, this "shareware" program, which can be downloaded free, via modem, from computer bulletin boards (a voluntary payment of $29 is requested), is not the fastest to use, but it is the only one that can compute the annualized return on a sin-

gle investment or your entire portfolio, as well as before- and after-tax returns on investments, taking into account the effect of dividends, stock splits, capital gains distributions, and other factors.

TAX PREPARATION

Tax software does away with the tedious sums, countless calculations, and math errors that make April so taxing. It lets you revise your return in seconds if you discover overlooked deductions or income. It allows you to experiment with different combinations of depreciation, expensing, and Keogh or IRA contributions to save the most tax. Best of all, it frees you for the more lucrative task of tax planning, answering such questions as the tax consequences of buying or leasing a car, investing in rental property, or rolling over a pension plan distribution.

If you use the short Forms 1040EZ or 1040A, you can probably prepare your return as efficiently and more economically with a calculator. Even if you file a regular Form 1040, you probably don't need a tax program if your return is fairly straightforward. But if you find yourself bogged down in such technical traps as depreciation, business schedules, partnership distributions, or five-year averaging, tax software may be a good investment.

Tax software performs two functions:

- storing and organizing your income and expense records
- using this information to prepare your return or analyze tax strategies

Financial record-keeping programs may be combined with a tax preparation program. Not only do you get more for your money with these programs, but you need to enter your financial data only once.

Make sure the program you buy is a final release, incorporating the latest tax law. Find out whether the program is updated annually or if you must purchase a new program each year.

Although the major tax programs are far from being clones, they all offer certain basic features:

- **Selecting the right forms.** If you don't know a Schedule E from a Form 2106, one of the brightest benefits of tax software is its ability to determine which forms you'll need. The software asks you a series of questions and from your answers lists the forms to be completed. When you're done, the program checks to see if you've been thorough and tells you when a form seems incomplete.
- **Matching the right number to the right line.** The program lets you select a tax item, such as church contributions, from a list and carries the dollar amount you enter to the right line of the right form.
- **Mathematical accuracy.** Never try to beat a computer at chess or arithmetic. With tax software, math errors are as impossible as a simplified tax code.
- **Internal consistency.** That $2,532 capital gain on Schedule D will show up where it's supposed to—on line 13 of the Form 1040—as $2,532, not $2,352 or some other mutation of the correct figure.
- **Spotting omissions.** To claim a child care credit, it's not enough to enter the amount you spent. Your software will tell you that the name and identification number of the child care provider are also required. Any time you leave a form undone, the program flags the problem.
- **Technical advice.** At a minimum, you get the IRS instruction booklet on-line, with specific form and line instructions keyed to those places on the screen. The

amount of additional advice you can count on varies.

▪ **Tax forms.** No more last-minute trips to the library for forms the IRS never sent you. They're all in your computer. These programs also print replicas of the Form 1040 and computer substitutes of other forms. If you have a laser printer, you can print forms that look just like the IRS versions, with your tax information already typed in.

▪ **Importing financial data.** You'll save hours at tax time if your tax information is already stored in a cash management program. The tax program can read your income and deductions from your checkbook files and transfer that data directly to your tax return. Make sure the program you choose supports your cash management program. For example, Turbotax imports data from Quicken and Managing Your Money.

▪ **Auditing.** When you've finished, the program checks for inconsistent or incomplete items, which could draw unwanted attention from the IRS. It also tells you if a deduction is higher than the national average.

These programs prepare federal returns only. A separate state tax package generally runs about $50. Only one program, TurboTax, supports all forty-five states that levy personal income tax. If you pick another program, ask whether your state package is available. Some state returns are so simple, however, that filling them out takes less time than loading the state program. It may be worth the extra cost, though, if you live in a state like California, where the tax rules differ significantly from federal law.

Leading tax preparation programs include

▪ *Andrew Tobias's TaxCut* (MECA, 800-288-MECA): This software features an excellent tutorial that teaches you how to use the program, an electronic "expert" that dispenses tax advice as you move through the forms, a guarantee of accuracy (or the company will pay the negligence penalty), and programs for ten states.

- *TurboTax* (Chipsoft, 619-453-8722): This best-selling tax software leads you step by step through the tax preparation process and also offers a quick tutorial, drop-down menus for ease in moving between forms, and returns for every state with an income tax (more than any other program).
- *Swiftax* (Timeworks, 708-948-9206): Featuring an excellent Help system, this program also comes with a tax book full of good tax advice and beats the others to market in the late fall with an early-bird edition that can be cheaply updated in January.
- *J. K. Lasser's Your Income Tax Software* (Simon & Schuster Software, Prentice-Hall Mail Order, Route 59 at Brookhill Drive, West Nyack, NY 10994-9901): Accompanied by the J. K. Lasser income tax book, this package interviews you to lead you to the forms you need, offers tax tips, automatically transfers data from supporting forms to the 1040, checks for omissions, and supports twenty-four states.

INFORMATION SERVICES

It's almost impossible to sift through, much less absorb, all the financial data available these days. Subscribing to an information service, however, provides a rapid way to obtain data pertinent to your investment goals. For example, you may want recent stock prices for a certain industry. To achieve this, you can spend a lot of time doing manual research, or you can use a computerized information service.

You can't beat the convenience. If you don't have time to mull over your investments during the workday, no problem. Information services "never close." You can research over the weekend, place your order Sunday night, and a broker will execute your trade when the market opens Monday morning. No playing phone tag with your broker, no waiting on hold.

To use an information service, you need a modem and the service's communications software. You subscribe by paying a onetime password fee. After that your monthly bill depends on how much time you use the service. Pay particular attention to these usage fees—they shouldn't exceed 1.5 percent of your portfolio annually.

Before choosing an information service, decide what kind of data you need. You can use these services for stock quotes, detailed historical pricing information, and information on the economic conditions underlying market trends, industries that are faring well, and specific stocks that look promising.

Also consider whether it's worth the cost. Typical on-line subscribers own some $150,000 worth of stocks or bonds and trade about once a week. If you're in doubt, I suggest subscribing for a few months to see if the benefits outweigh the fees.

The major financial information services are

- Dow Jones/News Retrieval (800-221-7700, ext. 577L): The leading service, consisting of thirty-five data bases, provides you with financial news, current quotes on stocks and other investments, fundamental data on over 4,300 companies, financial information on 9,400 public companies, earnings forecasts for 3,000 U.S. companies, a weekly survey of U.S. money markets and foreign exchange trends, and on-line trading through Fidelity Investors Express of Boston.

- CompuServe (800-848-8990): Developed to meet the needs of investors and business executives, this service owned by H & R Block offers current quotes on stocks and other financial instruments, fundamental information on more than 3,000 companies from Standard & Poor's, commodity newsletters, the Value Line data base of 1,700 major companies, and on-line stock trading with Quick & Reilly.
- GEnie (800-638-9636): No special software is needed for this service, which offers a wide range of business and financial services, letting you buy stocks, bonds, and mutual funds, as well as providing professional financial advice and historical reports on various investments.
- Warner (800-626-4634/201-489-1580): Designed for the financial community, this service features on-line trading with Charles Schwab & Co. and a rich fund of historical information of value in analyzing stocks.

All of the above information services provide current historical pricing, corporate statistics, earnings reports, stock quotes, and financial news. An added bonus for the time-pressed—you can download this information directly onto your portfolio management or spreadsheet program.

Less comprehensive, but much cheaper, financial information can be obtained from Prodigy (800-PRODIGY), which offers partial access to the Dow Jones/News Retrieval System (fifteen-minute delay), reports on companies in the news, research reports, and financial articles.

For stock quotes only, DTN Wall Street and Telemet's

Radio Exchange (800-368-2078) offer delayed quotes for about $35 a month.

ON-LINE TRADING

You can buy and sell stocks from your home with an on-line discount brokerage service. Although this saves commissions, you generally pay for on-line time and access fees. One thing you can't do by computer, though, is specify which shares of a block you want to sell in order to minimize taxable gains.

Three information utilities offerings this service are Dow Jones/News Retrieval, CompuServe, and Prodigy. Each utility orders through a particular brokerage firm, and you must open an account with that firm before trading. You can also trade on-line through Charles Schwab & Co. if you buy Schwab's Equalizer software (800-654-1444).

Chapter 10

Rapid Record Keeping for Tax Time

Good record keeping is not quantum mechanics. All you need is determination and a dose of common sense. You don't have to know a debit from a credit, and you don't need ledgers and double-entry journals. Something less sophisticated will probably do, unless you own your own business or corporation. In that case find an accountant or bookkeeper to establish a set of books for your business.

Your file cabinet is the best place to store tax records. Simply tossing in your records, however, will *not* do. Instead, sort them into categories and drop them into labeled file folders. If you favor the shoebox method, use labeled envelopes.

You should have the following categories:

Income (wages, inter-
   est/dividends, etc.).
Exemptions (cost of
   shelter, food, cloth-
   ing, etc.)

Medical expenses
Taxes
Interest
Contributions

Child care	Travel
Business expenses	Major purchases
Automobile (one for each car)	Miscellaneous

If your finances are more diversified, you may want to add the following:

Home and home improvements	Deeds
Rental property	Insurance
Escrow papers and mortgages	Legal and accounting
Investments	

The above categories are the most universal and should cover most of your income and expenses. Everyone's life and work are unique, however. If yours includes anything from annuities to zero-coupon bonds, feel free to add those as well.

SIMPLIFY YOUR TAXES

According to the IRS, it takes four hours and eight minutes to prepare a Form 1040 with itemized deductions. It takes *five hours and fifty-four minutes* just to get your records together. You can shave a few minutes off this time, however, by taking the following steps:

- File your receipts by category as previously advised. Never separate receipts by month. When it comes time to total your medical expenses, you want them all in one place—not scattered throughout twelve files.
- Don't leave your canceled checks wrapped inside your monthly bank statements. Sort your checks,

discarding those for nondeductible items. File your bank statements separately and keep them for three years.

- Staple canceled checks for deductible expenses to their related receipts.
- Don't pay cash for tax-deductible expenses. Write a check or flash a credit card instead.
- If you do a lot of business travel or entertaining, consider getting a separate credit card to use exclusively for these expenses. The monthly total will be the amount deductible. No need to trudge through your statements, separating business from personal expenses.
- If you do pay cash, get a receipt.
- Make a note of what you purchased if it's not clear from the receipt. Do the same with canceled checks, using the memo line in the lower left-hand corner to explain the purchase.

Keep only the current year's records in the income and expense categories. When you've finished your taxes, file those records with the tax return in another part of your cabinet.

WHAT RECORDS TO KEEP

You want to keep every receipt, check, cash register tape, and charge slip for *tax-deductible* items. Don't make judgments about deductibility on the run, however. Stuff every scrap of paper into your pocket or purse, and sort them when you get home. If a document fits into more than one category—for example, a home loan statement showing both interest and taxes—photocopy it or put a note behind one of the categories referring to where it can be found.

There's no need to keep a daily journal. The exceptions are for business mileage and the business use of a computer or cellular telephone if you're an employee. In these cases a log book detailing business use is a must. For business driving, keep the log in your car and write down the mileage and the purpose of your trip each time you hit the road on business.

If you entertain clients, I recommend entering in your appointment book the restaurant name, price of the meal, and the name of the person entertained.

The list of documents you should keep for tax purposes is far too long to print here. The complete list can be found in chapter 45 of *The Money Income Tax Handbook* by Mary L. Sprouse.

STOCKS, BONDS, AND MUTUAL FUNDS

Stock tips and "Wall Street Week" are fine. But well-organized investment records alone can dramatically improve your profits. By tracking the performance of your investments, you can weed out those that aren't meeting your financial goals, not to mention minimize taxes when it comes time to sell.

Luckily, the paper load is light. For all three types of investment, save the confirmation slip showing the number of shares you bought and what you paid for them. If you buy a bond, the slip also shows any accrued interest you paid to the seller. Suppose, for example, that the last time the bond paid interest was four months ago, and the next interest payment is due in two months. You would pay the seller four months' interest—the amount the bond earned while the seller was still the owner—because you'll receive the full six months' worth of interest two months from now.

Also keep the following:

- **Mutual funds**

  - Forms 1099-DIV showing dividends and capital gain distributions
  - Cumulative year-end statements showing amounts of dividends reinvested (or monthly statements if they're not cumulative)
  - Copies of any letters instructing your broker to sell a specific block of shares bought on a particular date or between certain dates. In a rising market, this tactic lets you sell the costly shares you bought most recently, postponing tax on the cheaper shares. (If you don't identify which shares you're selling, the IRS assumes you sold the earliest shares you bought)

- **Stocks**

  - Year-end dividend reinvestment statements
  - Forms 1099-DIV showing ordinary, capital gain, and nontaxable dividends
  - Copies of letters to broker confirming instructions to sell a specific block of shares (if this information isn't noted on broker's transaction slip)
  - Transaction slip showing number of shares sold and the amount you realized, less broker's commission
  - Form 1099-S showing total sales proceeds from stock sold

- **Bonds**

  - Forms 1099-INT showing interest earned
  - Transaction slip showing date bond was sold or redeemed and amount realized
  - Form 1099-S showing total proceeds from sale or redemption

INVESTMENT EXPENSES

The costs of producing taxable investment income may be deducted as miscellaneous itemized deductions, subject to the 2 percent of adjusted gross income limitation. Keep all receipts for the following deductible investment expenses:

- Accounting fees to keep a record of investment income
- Appraisal, insurance, mailing, restoration, and safekeeping fees of collectibles bought with a profit motive
- Clerical or secretarial wages paid to care for or manage your investments
- Custodian fees for holding shares, collecting and reinvesting cash dividends, and record keeping
- Investment counselor or management fees
- Investment publications, books, and newsletters that relate to investments you own
- Safety deposit box rent if the box is used to store stock certificates, bonds, and investment-related documents
- Travel and transportation to inspect income-producing property or to seek investment advice (but *not* travel to investigate property, attend investment conventions or seminars, or attend shareholder meetings)

CIRCULAR FILE

The most satisfying way to cut clutter is to throw out worthless paper. In general, if you don't need a record for tax purposes, don't save it. For example, you can discard all canceled checks for personal expenses, such as groceries, utilities (unless you have a home office), and your *Reader's Digest* subscription.

You can routinely toss the following items:

- Credit card bills
- Credit card slips (for nondeductible purchases)
- Monthly statements from brokerage firms and mutual funds (once your cumulative year-end statement is received)
- Receipts for everyday purchases
- Pay stubs (once Form W-2 is received)
- Duplicate records (such as cash register receipt for medicine if you paid by check or credit card)
- Restaurant stubs, if not for business entertainment

DISPOSING OF RECORDS

How long must your tax records take up valuable space? The general rule is that receipts may be discarded three years from the date the return is filed or due (or two years from the date the tax was paid, whichever is later). For example, your 1991 taxes, which were due April 1992, are subject to audit until April 1995. *Note:* If you obtained an extension of the April 15 deadline, the three years are calculated from the extended due date.

The IRS has six years to come after you if you underreported your gross income by more than 25 percent. If you failed to file a return at all or filed one that's considered fraudulent, there's no time limit.

Some records should be kept longer than three years:

- **Major purchases.** Receipts for expensive items, such as jewelry and furniture, should be saved for as long as you own the items. You may need them to settle insurance claims in case of loss, theft, or other damage.
- **Medical records.** If you apply for health insurance coverage, the insurance company may ask for details of hospital and doctor visits from up to ten years back.

- **Investments.** Keep stock certificates, transaction slips (broker's purchase and sales statements), and dividend reinvestment information until stock is sold. Bearer bonds should be kept until maturity or the bonds are sold.
- **Real estate.** Property records must be kept from the date of purchase until at least three years after the date of sale. If you've deferred gain, however, or are taking advantage of the after-age-55 exclusion, records should kept for as long as they're needed to determine the basis of the original property and the property that replaced it.

For example, if you sell your first home and defer the gain by reinvesting in a more expensive property, save the escrow statements for the first home until you dispose of the second. If you again defer gain on the sale of the second home, retain escrow statements for *both* properties until you sell the third.

Save the following records indefinitely:

- *Home improvements:* The cost of a new roof, landscaping, kitchen renovation, central air-conditioning, and other improvements that increase the value of your home can be added to the purchase price to reduce your capital gain when you sell.

  Painting and repairs are considered maintenance, not improvements. You don't need to keep these receipts unless the work is part of a major remodeling (an improvement) or you're renting out your home.
- *Escrow or settlement statements:* These documents show recording and transfer taxes, closing costs, title insurance, and legal fees that can be added to your cost basis, thereby reducing your taxable gain.
- *Refinancing:* Points paid to refinance are amortized and deducted over the life of your loan. Other

fees paid to refinance are added to the cost of your property.

- *Form 2119, "Sale of Principal Residence":* If you postpone or exclude gain on the sale of your home, this form computes the cost basis of your replacement home.

■ **Self-employed business.** If you own a business, save the following records for six years:

- Accounts payable and accounts receivable ledgers
- Expired contracts
- Employee time reports
- Disability and sick benefit records
- Personnel files of former employees
- Forms W-4 "Withholding Tax Statements"
- Freight bills, manifests, shipping and receiving reports, and bills of lading

Keep payroll records, including canceled payroll checks, individual time reports, and earnings records, for *eight* years.

■ **Depreciable assets.** Proof of how much you paid for such items as a business automobile, computer, or office equipment, should be kept for as long as you have the asset plus three years.

■ **IRAs.** If you made deductible IRA contributions before tax reform, but your income and coverage by a qualified pension plan make your contributions partly or wholly nondeductible now, you must keep detailed records of your deductible and nondeductible contributions. For that reason make sure your nondeductible contributions are in a separate account.

You must save the following for each year you make nondeductible IRA contributions—otherwise you risk having to pay tax on your nondeductible contributions when you withdraw the money years from now:

- Your federal and state income tax returns
- Forms 5498, "Individual Retirement Account Information," sent by the institution holding the funds
- Forms 8606, "Nondeductible IRA Contributions, IRA Basis, and Nontaxable IRA Distributions"

All these records should be kept until three years after the funds are withdrawn:

▪ **Alternative minimum tax.** Keep records indefinitely for any year in which you pay alternative minimum tax. You may be able to claim a credit in future years. Ask your tax adviser exactly which records you may need later on.

▪ **Passive activity losses.** The current passive loss rules may restrict the amount you may deduct now. Passive losses are those you incur when you invest in a business you don't actively manage (for example, commercial real estate in which you are a limited partner). In that case, your unused losses are carried over until you have offsetting passive income or the property is sold. Keep supporting documents, such as partnership K-1s, until three years after your tax adviser informs you that your passive loss has been fully deducted.

▪ **Tax returns.** Keep copies of your tax returns forever. You may need to refer back to them in preparing subsequent returns if you have to pay alimony, sell business or investment property at a loss, or suffer a net operating loss. You may also need them for reasons that go beyond taxes, such as loan applications and divorce. If you don't have a copy of your tax return, ask the IRS to send you Form 4506, "Request for Copy of Tax Form."

Index